ACT III

X *X* *X* *X* *X*

YOUR
Anti-Retirement
PLAYBOOK

ACT III

YOUR
Anti-Retirement
PLAYBOOK

CECILIA WILLIAMS, Ph.D.
& PAULA WHITE, CPA, MBA

This book is meant to be a guide, a playbook for retirement and to leave the reader better informed about all the opportunities available to them in their Act III. However it is in no way intended to replace the advice of CPAs, financial planners and consultants, medical practitioners, health-care professionals, or any of the other professionals usually involved in advising retirees. The authors and publisher specifically disclaim any liability incurred from the use or application of the contents of this book.

Act III: Your Anti-Retirement Playbook.
Copyright © 2015 by Cecilia Williams and Paula White.

For information, address WAN Publishing, LLC at info@wanpublishing.com.

FIRST EDITION

Book design by GKS Creative

Library of Congress Cataloging-in-Publication Data
has been applied for.

978-0-9863989-0-2   US Edition

1. Retirement
2. Self-help (SEL021000 motivational SEL027000
       personal growth/success)

We dedicate this book to our parents. Though no longer with us, they remain our teachers and guides.

TABLE OF CONTENTS

FOREWORD

The third-act conflict leads us to a big scene, which the audience has been waiting for since the story began.
—HTTP://THESCRIPTLAB.COM

This book began one Sunday afternoon when the two of us were anticipating a break from teaching, consulting, and running our businesses. Having two weeks off from teaching was a rarity; rarer still were two weeks when both of us had the same opening in our schedules. "We can take a vacation!" we said in unison. As a general rule, we worked fifty- to seventy-hour workweeks and wore the weary faces of those whose only time off was to get a haircut or visit the dentist. We needed a vacation that would focus on relaxation, wouldn't drain our budget, and would be intensely fun.

"We need fun!" we told each other. "What can we do that is fun?"

The answer was more difficult than we had imagined. We liked going to the movies. We liked reading. We lived just blocks from the ocean. But what did we do for fun?

When the answer didn't come, we tried creative problem solving. You know—"If you won a million dollars today, what would you do?"

No answer.

"If you won a million dollars today and were in your twenties, what would you do?"

Worse than no answer, we couldn't even think of doing the last thirty years over again!

Then we tried again, "What if you were retired and had a million dollars, what would you do?"

That one struck home! We knew that the answer would affect the rest of our lives. Not quite ready for retirement, we were in the awkward ages, the late fifties where we were not looked upon as prime material by current and upcoming employers, but young enough that we couldn't order a senior breakfast without being "carded."

The truth is, we tried not to think about retirement; it was frightening. How would we, who couldn't decide how to take a two-week vacation, decide how to have a life of full-time leisure? How would we, who had little time to make up for financial setbacks, fund the dreams of retirement once we knew what they were? Would our health see us through or would we suffer the long illnesses we had witnessed in our parents? Both single and without children, who would take care of us?

We became curious about these two words: retirement and fun. For us, they seemed connected. We didn't buy into the happy group sailing on a yacht with glasses of wine in hand and smiling with apparent joy while the sun set behind them. While the advertisement for health insurance, financial planning, or a cruise line would have us believe that the purchase of their product or service had led to this happy event, we still couldn't explain why they were happy. Still, absent of what people usually complain about—unhappy jobs, financial concerns, lack of time—being rid of the job and having time to rule your own days *should* bring happiness.

Shouldn't it?

We set out on a mission to guide ourselves and others through this time of transition. To learn more, we started attending seminars on retirement. We visited 55+ centers. We read reports on aging. And most importantly, we interviewed hundreds of retirees and hundreds of others still in the same awkward age we were in. We watched, we learned, we listened.

We also started learning more about fun. To learn more about fun, we started trying new things and then reflected upon why we considered them fun. We observed others having fun and noticed what was special in their approach. The results were fascinating and not what you will read about in any book about funding your retirement.

The more we learned, the more we discovered that it was impossible to talk about "retirement years" because each person interprets the word "retirement" differently. In the realities of financial setbacks, job losses, and a struggling and erratic economy, people are working much longer than they ever have before. In our interviews, people talked about their values, the relationships they wanted to keep, and the dreams they had yet to live. They talked about struggles they still had, their relationship with God, their health, and financial concerns.

Improvements in health care make it possible to live twenty to twenty-five years beyond "the working years" before health becomes a restrictive consideration. Some people said, "I'm retired, but I would never give up working because I love what I do." For some, retirement means leaving the workforce and never working for someone else again. For others, it means being grandparents and spending more time with the kids. And for one interviewee, it meant opening up a bed and breakfast in Tuscany.

In fact, the common thread was not the ability to draw social security payments, but instead, our interviewees were engaged in a transition—for many, the biggest transition in their lives. What is more important, people in this stage were reevaluating their lives, their purpose, their relationships, and their dreams in order to prepare for their next phase of life. Some transitioned conscientiously; others did not. Our interviews revealed that what we call retirement is a transition period with some common themes. One may reach this stage at many different ages. It is not defined as the day you reach sixty-five or the day you are cheered on with your "retirement farewell."

This book delves into the seven themes of transition identified through our research. We invite you to explore these themes with us. Take time to read slowly and work through the self-exploration activities. This book is not a novel or a chance to practice your speed-reading skills. It is a workbook filled with activities designed to help you in your personal transition. The transition is a process. It is an unfolding of your renewed potential. But, you cannot experience that renewal unless you do the work.

The transition is a process. It is an unfolding of your renewed potential. In this stage of life, people start dropping their "have-to's" and, if they are successful, start living lives of choice.

In this stage of life, people start dropping their "have-to's" and, if they are successful, start living lives of choice. Surprisingly, the choice is not necessarily related to finances. A life choice may mean staying employed. It may mean traveling the world and teaching English. It may mean turning a hobby into a life purpose. It may mean finding relevance as a family member. So many transitions are made in this stage that it deserves to be called more than a word that implies that one has simply stopped and withdrawn.

We decided to call this stage of life "Act III" because, in a play, it is the act where all that has gone on before comes to a climax. We call the people experiencing this stage "Third Act-ors" (TAs for short). Third Act-ors are far from done! TAs don't have time to waste on getting approval from others. TAs have experience and wisdom that the world needs and have a burning desire to share it. TAs have "been there; done that" and now, want to do things that are unique and driven by their own passion. TAs have the patience to listen and the power to shift and guide. TAs want to live life at its fullest. TAs have a voice.

This book is written for Third Act-ors. It is written so that you may become the fulfillment of your Act III and live a life that is fully chosen. By preparing and guiding yourself through these priceless years, it is our hope that you will find them the most rewarding of your life. We hope that you will dare to challenge your own assumptions, so that you will not "spend" these years, but fully use and treasure them.

We hope you have fun.

ACKNOWLEDGMENTS

Our book began when we asked each other, "What is fun?"

In our quest for "fun," we attended the 2013 Writers Forum at the University of Phoenix, San Diego Campus. At this event, we met many writers and presenters, one of whom encouraged us to attend the La Jolla Writers Conference. It was at this wonderful conference that we received the personal guidance that helped us develop and propose the concept of this book to the conference faculty. We want to acknowledge and thank those who heard our first ideas and encouraged us to develop the book: Antoinette Kuritz, Warren Lewis, Bill Gladstone, Helen Zimmerman, and Glen Yeffeth.

Special thanks to our friends Diane Blankenship, Sandy Huppenbauer, Taleed El-Sabawi, Janelle Shuster and Dermot Rodgers who read the rough drafts of our manuscript and provided us with valuable feedback. Our appreciation also goes out to Anthony Ellis and Nan MacIsaac; we cannot thank you enough for your friendship and professional advice. We were blessed with Bill and Jan Salas who provided detailed thoughts to the final work.

We want to acknowledge Antoinette Kuritz for sharing her expertise in book development and PR; Jared Kuritz for supporting us in social media and marketing; Mary Altbaum for her detailed skills as our copy editor; and Gwyn Kennedy Snider for her cover design and interior layout.

And most importantly, we want to thank the many people who shared their life stories, concerns, insights and joys as they transition into their Act III.

INTRODUCTION

How We Became Who We Are

If you are currently entering Act III, chances are you are part of a generation known as "baby boomers." As such, you grew up in a competitive environment that encouraged optimism, a hope for a better world, and a desire to change the world.

One of the first words we learned in our elementary school reader was "w-o-r-k" and through education, we prepared for the day that we would become productive members of society. Eighty-nine percent of baby boomers completed high school and pursued colleges and universities at a rate unheard of in previous generations. For baby boomers, higher education was not an option for the privileged few; it was a birthright. We lived our young-adult lives to the fullest, becoming involved in causes for peace, challenging society's rules, and exploring our innermost nature.

We were bound by very little. Birth control pills entered the market, allowing us to delay our families and extend our time of exploration and self-indulgence. We entered an employment market that believed in investing in us. And why wouldn't they invest? Business was growing and new graduates offered a pool of educated talent. Our first jobs were filled with training opportunities. Educational and training vendors entered the market to teach us how to supervise employees, write better business letters, get people to "yes," learn how to dress for success, learn computers, and make a fortune in real estate. In our spare time, we learned to play golf, strike yoga poses, fly airplanes, and play the stock market. We believed if we were not learning, we would fall behind. We were warriors, ready to take on the world, change society, conquer evil, and build the future of America.

As we became successful, we acquired status symbols. Montblanc pens were visibly displayed as medals of honor. Houses were purchased with huge mortgages. Women sought to have it all—building a career and raising a family. Sometimes, changes were made in the family structure to make it all work. Men discovered that they, too, could change a diaper. But there was stress with all of the colliding forces that drove us to define ourselves. Divorces became commonplace; families disintegrated and evolved as extended families. Societal norms were up for challenge, but the desire for material wealth and personal growth remained strong. We still had our sights on living the American Dream—with a few slight changes. This was our birthright!

Just as we were experiencing signs of being in reach of our goals, the world changed. Once having been the cared-for child, we became caregivers to our aging parents. We were the "sandwich" generation, caring for children while taking on responsibilities for our parents. At first, it was okay. We had it in the budget to buy some extra groceries or buy dad a motorized scooter. We started to learn about life in a new way as our parents now grew frail and dependent.

Then, for many of us, the nightmare began.

The economic crash of 2001 hit baby boomers in their prime earning years. We looked on in despair as we saw the twin towers fall in New York City. The disaster reflected the fall in our personal lives as the economic downturn began to take its toll.

Known as the Second Great Depression, baby boomers were faced with a situation that hard work and education could not dispel. In 2001, the growth of the dot-com industry reversed, coming in line with companies' true worth, but reversing the somewhat artificial growth of the 1990s to which baby-boom investments were committed. One of our interviewees remembers the day she lost a corporate client for whom she had just made a major bid for a customer service project. "I'm sorry, but we won't be buying your services next year; ten thousand employees were laid off this morning . . . everything is on hold."

Figure 1 shows the drop in the percent of people employed as we entered the twenty-first century. While this drop is impressive, it is even more so

3

when one considers that baby boomers were in their prime earning years, the oldest baby boomer being fifty-five years of age at the start of the decade-long decline. Merchants who enjoyed growth during the economic boom felt the impact of dropping sales as baby boomers cashed out retirement savings and suffered the loss of lifetime savings.

Figure 1: Percent of US Civilian Working-Age Population Employed 1995–2012

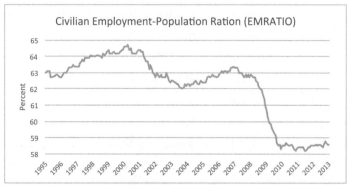

Civilian Employment-Population Ration (EMRATIO)

U.S. Department of Labor: Bureau of Labor Statistics (FRED)

What Does This Mean To Those Entering Act III?

In this book, we assume that everything that has built the character of the TAs is good. Baby boomers have been shaken, but they have also had an opportunity to review their values. They have continued to rely on their strengths and found more strength than they ever knew they had. With optimism and an unyielding commitment to learning, they have mastered new industries and moved into second, third, and fourth careers. They have returned to school.

Humbled by changes beyond their control, they have thrown out symbols of success and opted for lives of purpose. As one baby boomer said during a job interview: "It is one thing to have moved up the corporate ladder once—but to have been successful, failed, and pulled oneself back up . . . well, that is real success, real character."

Real character is what we have entering into Act III. We are educated and competitive. We love to learn; we love to achieve. Since our youth, we have wanted to make a difference in the world. We have been seasoned by hardships and challenges. We have learned from the lives of those who have gone before us. We are unlikely to accept "not working" as our only goal. In some cases, to consider anything other than gainful employment is not an option. The definition of success has broadened to more than a monetary standard. We will test the assumptions of aging as we have tested the assumption of every life stage so far. We want our wisdom to make a difference. We want our lives to have purpose.

We have just begun to live!

ACT III Model: An Overview

When starting this book, we considered the areas that we would need to cover in order to capture the essential areas of Act III. We recognized that life itself was rarely balanced. Certainly, there were times in our lives when the role of caregiver and business owner had exhausted any hope of getting a full night's sleep—much less exploring interests. At times, relationships took center stage. At other times, we pursued an interest that was so captivating, we would toss away responsibility, dismissing day-to-day demands as an inconsequential annoyance. Sometimes, it seemed like we "lost pieces" of ourselves as we gave time away to work, parents, and children. In fact, an all too common theme among those longing for retirement is that they look forward to a time when they can find their pieces again.

In our interviews with TAs, we created a structure so we and our readers could develop, explore, and never lose pieces of ourselves again. This structure is the backbone of this book. We were not just authors of this structure. We have used it to explore our own lives. Walking through this structure has helped us identify what we want in our lives going forward. We hope that you will join us in that walk.

Figure 2: The Structure of Act III

Exploring Interests

Staying in Touch with Technology

Recognizing and Fulfilling Dreams

Work and Financial Management

YOUR ACT III

Relationships

Nurturing the Soul

Health

The structure shown in *Figure 2* contains elements in the foreground and background. The foreground includes recognizing and fulfilling dreams, work and financial management, and relationships. The background supports these three sections. This structure does not mean that our lives are defined subjects with barriers separating them from one another, but instead a free-flowing set of topics that combine and interrelate to create life's experiences. For example, work certainly impacts financial management; financial management provides the means for accessing technology; accessing technology allows you, through social media, to connect easily with friends and relatives. A benefit of healthy relationships is good health, both mental and physical; with good mental health, dreams can be recognized and fulfilled while exploring new interests that will add to our purpose while we nurture our soul. The intertwining action of these areas will create an energy that expands to evolve and enhance the quality of life. What keeps this action going is our positive can-do attitudes; what stops this action is our negative attitudes.

As we transition into Act III we are not entering "retirement." The very word evokes a false impression. The Oxford Dictionary defines retirement as the act of "ending one's working or professional career" and lists as synonyms the words *pullback, pullout, recession, retreat,* and *withdrawal.* A second definition describes "a place of seclusion or privacy."

The Act III we propose is not about leaving work or continuing work, and it is certainly not about pulling back. Rather, it is about the time in our life when we can make choices, given the flexibility created by wisdom, lifetime skills, financial foundation, and an acute understanding that now there can be no excuses for not living a life in balance, joy, and purpose.

The time for Act III is up to you; we hope it will be soon.

So let's begin your adventure.

Exploring Interests

A man is not old until regrets take the place of dreams.
—JOHN BARRYMORE

AT FIRST, WE FOUND IT DIFFICULT to identify our interests. It seemed that we were doing things because we had to in order to make a living or fulfill our responsibilities to others. It wasn't that we didn't like what we did, it was just that we *had* to do those things. We noticed that we both had been saying "I must" and "I have to." These phrases more than peppered our speech; they smothered it. Then we came upon an idea that changed our lives. We experimentally changed just those two phrases. We mindfully exchanged that part of our scripts to "We choose to." The next morning, instead of saying, "We have to go to work," we said, "We choose to go to work today." "We choose to work in our professions." "We choose to be helpful to our clients today." We both did this and soon realized that we did find pleasure in most of these activities! There were other choices we could make, but we "chose" these. At other times, we realized that we did not have to make that choice, and found ways to substitute that choice or toss it all together. At first it was an effort to say, "We choose," but as the weeks passed we realized what a great life we were choosing to live. Now we felt in control. This was just the beginning of recognizing and fulfilling dreams.

Recognizing and Fulfilling Dreams

The two worksheets in this section will introduce you to the dreams and interests you have already chosen, and help you realize that you have already had golden moments of living your dreams. As you recognize your dream moments, you will be able to increase the choices you have made in this direction, finding more options in fulfilling your dreams. The first technique is mind mapping.

Act III Dream Builder: Part I

Mind mapping is a time-honored way of visual thinking and problem solving, and it was made popular by Tony Buzan in a 1970s BBC TV series called *Use Your Head*. There are several versions of this visual technique, but the main purpose of mind mapping is to use your visual thinking abilities to map together thoughts without the constraints of sequential thinking. The technique we will use is relatively simple.

We suggest that you do this activity as a private, personal exercise. By performing the activity alone and not in the presence of others, you avoid the possibility of having someone make suggestions or critiquing "your" list of interests. Start with a piece of paper (the larger the better). Many people like to use different colored pens so that they can put similar themes in the same color. We suggest that you skip any attempts at refinement the first time you work on your map so that you do not hamper the flow of creativity. You can always go back and make your map more artistic later.

Start by putting a circle in the middle of the paper and in the center of the circle write, "What I like to do." Create spokes radiating from this center circle like spokes of a wagon wheel. As you think of each new area of interest, place it at the end of the spoke in a new circle. If you wrote down "relax" in a circle, expand that concept by adding spokes and circles to it that include "sunbathe next to the pool," "walk on the beach," "golf," "watch bowling on TV," "watch old movies," or "solve crossword puzzles." Do not worry about whether or not you are doing these things now or in the past. You are pulling out of your mind activities you have found pleasurable.

Ideas that are related can be connected with lines. Connect at will without worrying about the neatness of your map. Do not self-critique in this process but do work as quickly as you can; expand ideas but do not edit them.

Exercise Example 1 shows an example of a mind map. Yours can look very different so long as the general concept holds. Now go mapping and come back when you are done.

Exercise Example 1: Example of A Mind Map

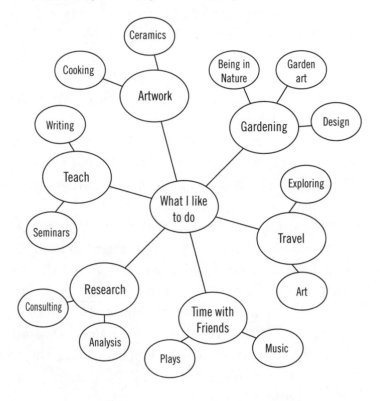

Mind Mapping Exercise

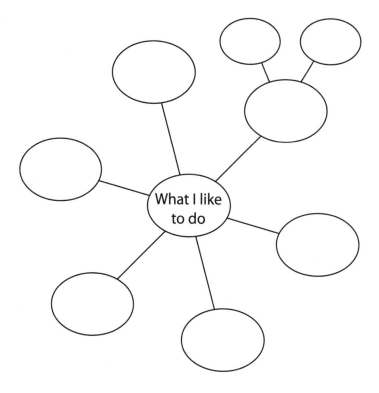

What I like to do

Now that your map is done, did you have any surprises? If so, write them down here.

Interests and Activities That Surprised Me

_____

_____

_____

_____

_____

_____

_____

_____

_____

_____

_____

_____

_____

_____

_____

_____

_____

_____

_____

Did you find, on reflection, any interests or activities that "should have" been there? There may be reasons why you left them out.

List them here:

Activities and Interests I Didn't Include

_____

_____

_____

_____

_____

_____

_____

_____

_____

_____

_____

_____

_____

_____

_____

_____

What's on your list that others would find surprising? Why?

List them here:

Interests or Activities That Would Surprise Others

_____

_____

_____

_____

_____

_____

_____

_____

_____

_____

_____

_____

_____

_____

_____

_____

_____

_____

_____

What's not on your list that others would be surprised are not there? Why?

List them here:

My Surprises for Others (Excluded from My Mind Map)

_____

_____

_____

_____

_____

_____

_____

_____

_____

_____

_____

_____

_____

_____

_____

_____

Congratulations on stepping toward recognizing your dreams.

Reflect on your mind map. Can you consider a commitment to something that you identified, but are no longer engaged in doing? Is there a "secret" interest that you would consider exploring if you felt there was greater "approval" from others? Are there areas you are committing time to, but do not give you pleasure today? If so, why are you still doing them (i.e., what other benefits are there to these activities)?

Now we want to find more opportunities to expand on these glimpses of your interests. Let's explore your interests so we can find insights to your dreams.

Recognizing and Fulfilling Dreams

The difficulty lies not so much in developing new ideas
as in escaping from old ones...
—JOHN MAYNARD KEYNES

ACT III IS ABOUT "TRANSITION." During our interviews, we found that many people were stuck. Some people were stuck in a life they did not want to continue. For example, they held on to jobs they hated because they "needed to work" until they retired. They did not realize that dreams did not have to wait until retirement. Others had entered retirement who had not yet decided what they wanted to do with their time. They were stuck thinking that old dreams were no longer available, or worse, their preconceived values and ideas of retirement relegated them to "age appropriate behavior." Let's take a look at two examples of the "stuck."

Caitlyn's Story

Caitlyn was a successful financial broker who had used the wisdom gained on her job to make the right investment decisions for her own personal life. In Caitlyn's youth, she had dreamed of being a marine biologist, but found that it just wasn't "a practical way" to live. In spite of her success as a broker, Caitlyn didn't believe that she was working with her personal values. She felt pressured to sell the investments that her company supported and did not feel that she had enough freedom to suggest investments more in line with her clients' interest or understanding of investment. The more Caitlyn's retirement fund grew, the stronger her feeling that she just "couldn't stand one more day working for someone else." Caitlyn retired at age fifty, secure in the fact that her savings would see her through.

But once Caitlyn retired, she didn't know what to do. At first, she tinkered around the house, and redesigned the backyard. She repainted her bedroom, changed out the carpeting, and cleaned out the garage. To her surprise, she wasn't feeling as happy as she thought she would be. Sure, she didn't feel stressed. She slept in until eight o'clock in the morning and was doing things she liked to do. But she also felt that she was aging too soon. She lacked purpose, and what is more, she realized that her whole life had been about getting to retirement. Was this all there was? At fifty-one, she had half her life ahead of her and had come to realize that she had never really lived.

Ken's Story

Ken retired as a result of layoff. His entire life was a series of projects, jobs, and relationships that did not work out. He had been a high-end marketing communications specialist whose job skills were made obsolete by desktop publishing and other technologies. He did not keep up with his profession, believing that there would always be jobs for someone with his experience. He went on interview after interview but never received an offer at his pay grade. Because Ken had been so successful in earning a living, he did not learn the new technologies that his junior associates were embracing. He was trapped by his own view of his success. Because he believed that his goal should be to regain his former status, he did not take advantage of learning opportunities that "paid pennies." He continued to express anger at his former employer who had deprived him of his status and accepted short-term situations that never worked out. In reality, his victimhood created an unchangeable self-concept preventing him from exploring opportunities, taking chances, and living life to the fullest. So when you meet with Ken today, he is angry, negative, and pushes people, opportunities, and new adventures away. His focus is on survival and making sure his finances last until the end.

In contrast to these two stories, consider Joann.

Joann's Story

Joann worked for a marketing firm as an international product manager. She was very successful in her career. Fluent in multiple languages, she travelled worldwide on business, representing her client companies in a variety of cultures and settings. Like Ken, technology changed her profession. She no longer needed to travel in order to make proposals or meet with clients because computer technology allowed her and her clients to give online presentations. Most of the countries she visited started to develop employees who were fluent in English. Change not only impacted Joann, it impacted her industry and her employer. It was no surprise to Joann that her firm dissolved as the client list dwindled.

Joann started working at a local gift shop. While the pay was minimal, the store was close to home and the work schedule allowed her to explore opportunities during the day. One day, Joann reflected on the fact that she could no longer get the special chocolate truffles she used to purchase from a chocolatier in Belgium. To fill in her free time, she started experimenting with recipes and even took a class on candy making offered at a local community college. Soon, her skills in candy making grew, and she started her own class, specializing in teaching her own line of Belgium-influenced truffles. On occasion, she would sell a batch of her line to students who, finding the art too complex, were more than happy to pay premium price for the product.

Joann frequently shared her truffles with the shop owner. One day, the owner asked her if she would be interested in selling her truffles on consignment within the shop. After discussing the nature of the display, and special requirements for temperature, Joann excitedly said, "yes." Joann hoped the sales would help offset the rising cost of her baking needs.

One day, a gentleman walked into the shop and asked if her truffles could be packaged individually. Joann assumed he was looking for favors for wedding guests, so she said that she could package the candy in little gold mesh bags. She also offered to personalize the ribbon tie. She got an order for a thousand truffles on the spot. That sale was just the beginning. It turned out that the little truffle bags were not for a wedding, but for a major hotel chain that was looking for a branded touch for their penthouse guests worldwide. Joann does not need to work at the shop anymore. She is eighty-seven and still runs her company. Joann's story is not one of luck and timing. It is a story of not judging, but accepting opportunities in the moment. Joann, in reflection, realizes how everything fit together. She remembers the talks she had with the chocolatiers in Belgium, discussing ingredients and what made their chocolates special. The job she took in the shop at minimum wage was her training ground in the retail industry. The gold mesh bags that she suggested were the same design that she had made hundreds of times for fundraisers at her child's school. Her success was the result of saying "yes" to every opportunity without judgment or figuring out how it was all going to work out. She now knows being a chocolatier is part of her dream.

The following activity is designed to help you reflect on your dreams that you are quietly building. You may know your dream seeds as your talents, desires, gifts, or pleasures. Just as Joann's history had laid the groundwork for her future by training her how to respond to peoples' needs, how to market a product, and how to make great chocolate, you, too, could be building the foundation of your dreams without recognizing it.

So the next worksheet is for the second part of your Act III Dream Builder. Set judgment aside and have fun.

Act III Dream Builder: Part II

Return to the mind map you created in Act III Dream Builder: Part I and identify the major circles. For each major circle on the mind map, enter that as an "Area" on the Act III Dream Builder Worksheet shown later in this section. If you have smaller circles extending from any main concept, add the additional circle titles beneath the main concept that is already listed under "Area." You will repeat the form many times as you consider each area.

For each area, note the parts about the interest or activity that you do not want to continue and write that under the "Toss" caption. Then for that same area, write the elements that you want to continue under the "Hold (Continue)" caption. Under the "Add" caption, record the parts that you want to expand. Let's look at an example.

Cecilia demonstrated this activity using the circle in her mind map titled "Gardening." Here it is for you to see how the exercise unfolds.

Exercise Example 2: Cecilia's Act III Dream Builder Worksheet

AREA	TOSS	HOLD (CONTINUE)	ADD
Gardening	grass and mowing	simple/water-wise gardening	more fruit trees and organic vegetables
		composting and maintenance	knowledge about orchids and care of fruit trees
Garden: Art		ceramic art I have made	explore selling ceramic art
Garden: Design			explore coursework in landscape design
Being in nature		being in nature	

While gardening was already one of Cecilia's favorite activities, this exercise helped her understand that some changes in her yard would help her enjoy her pastime even more. It replaced expensive lawn maintenance with options that would increase her enjoyment and allow her to take care of the yard for many years to come. The organic vegetables and new fruit trees would supply her table with fresh organic produce that would make the utility bills worth the effort. Cecilia likes to refer to her garden as "the Act III revision." Everything in it brings her pleasure. In addition, Cecilia started making ceramic mushrooms to build a fantasy garden full of fairies and scenes. Children love to visit this garden and their parents soon asked

Cecilia to help them create gardens of their own. Currently Cecilia is challenged by the demand for ceramic mushrooms and fairy furniture. Typical of mind-map planning, not every item needs to be completed for fulfillment. Cecilia, having developed her own unique style, no longer felt the need to take a formal course in landscape design.

Now, it is your turn to create your Act III Dream Builder: Part II Worksheet. Be as specific as you can in this exercise and do not throw away your worksheets as you will be using them again in a future section. Don't rush things, take your time—you will have many sheets.

Act III Dream Builder: Part II Worksheet

AREA	TOSS	HOLD (CONTINUE)	ADD

As you finish each Act III Dream Builder: Part II Worksheet, note how the "Hold (Continue)" and "Add" columns are the basis for your dreams. Sit back and reflect on these dreams. Do not critique them, just reflect on them. Now in the "Hold (Continue)" column, circle the three that are most important to you. These are the activities that, at this moment, are at the top of your Act III Dream Builder list. Set aside a time each month to review your list and update your top three activities. By continuously working toward your dreams, you are living some of your dreams now instead of waiting for some time in the future.

Living your dreams now instead of waiting for some time in the future can have many benefits. It allows us to test the things we think we want. Consider Christine who had looked forward to retirement as a time when she would take up quilting as a hobby. Quilting had an emotional connection as it was an activity her mother enjoyed. In fact, she had converted part of her garage into a quilting workroom. Then she took a quilting course offered by a local fabric store and knew, after her first set of wonky placemats, that quilting was not as relaxing as she thought; it had no place in her Act III. Christine instead discovered she needed to be much more active in her leisure. Now, she is looking for ways to learn how to use her photography interests. She joined a Meetup.com group of photographers and discovered that she not only liked developing her skills, but enjoys the people and places that this group has introduced.

Summary

Many times we do not fulfill our dreams because we have not stated them. You may be surprised that once you have identified a key area, you will see more opportunities that will help you to experience that dream.

Before continuing on in this book, take a few minutes to reflect on your interests and dreams. Below, list what you feel are your "top three" areas identified in your Act III Dream Builder: Part II Worksheet. You will be using these in the last section.

Dreams

1.＿＿＿＿＿＿＿＿＿＿＿＿＿＿＿＿＿＿＿＿＿＿＿＿＿＿

2.＿＿＿＿＿＿＿＿＿＿＿＿＿＿＿＿＿＿＿＿＿＿＿＿＿＿

3.＿＿＿＿＿＿＿＿＿＿＿＿＿＿＿＿＿＿＿＿＿＿＿＿＿＿

SECTION 3

Staying in Touch
with Technology

Everything that can be invented has been invented.
—CHARLES H. DUELL, COMMISSIONER,
US PATENT OFFICE, 1899

IMAGINE IF YOU HAD NOT KEPT UP with the technology developments of recent decades. The first cell phones were not introduced until the 1980s. Just watch a movie produced in that era and you will recall just how awkward those talk boxes were! The BlackBerry was introduced in 1999 with e-mail capability, and Personal Digital Assistants (PDAs) were introduced about the same time. GPS for emergency services was mandated by the US Federal Communications Commission (FCC) in order to locate 911 callers. Today, cell phones are like a central operating center. E-mails can be sent and received. Through add-in software, a video conference can be hosted and pictures of material viewed on the screen can be captured for historical files. Contacts can be updated, calendars put in sync, and alerts can remind you it is time to go to the dentist. Voice translators tell the GPS interface that you would like to locate that dentist and get directions. Options allow you to see a picture of the street and buildings, making sure you don't waste time parking in the wrong parking lot. While you are sitting in the dentist chair, the cell phone can charge using a solar back-up battery and notes from your tablet can be updated into your phone using your mobile hot spot.

Have you noticed how the news has changed lately? Popular morning shows feature sections on what is trending on social networks. Live news is supplemented by pictures taken by viewers' cell phones and tablets. Television networks are learning that news is not only what professionals research and report. That process is too slow. Today the "cloud" is the source of new information. "News" helps to verify, consolidate, and explore the subject in-depth.

To borrow from the 1968 Virginia Slims commercial, we've "come a long way, baby!"

When it comes to technology, TAs tend to fall into one of three groups. A few are nonusers who may have a cell phone and can perform e-mail functions, and perhaps browse the Internet. Another group can text, access a social network site, and see digital pictures of their grandchildren.

Some in this group have discovered online video chats (usually set up by their adult children) and enjoy connecting with their family across the country, catching up on family news.

Very few keep up with the *latest* technology, integrating the capabilities of cell phones, tablets, personal computers, and the ever-growing library of apps and widgets that bring in new features and functions. Indeed, so many technologies seem to be emerging that it is hard to catch up. But there is more to the story: The issue is not the pace of technology, but the pace of our interest. It is too easy to fall into the trap of thinking that we have learned enough and that the newer advances are just bells and whistles. A few may even argue that technology has cut us off from real communications. In a *Saturday Night Live* comedy script featuring comedienne Betty White, she explained that she had learned about Facebook and "it sounds like a huge waste of time." Our laughter betrays the fact that we are on her side thinking new trends are not important.

The issue is not the pace of technology, but the pace of our interest. It is too easy to fall into the trap of thinking that we have learned enough and that the newer advances are just bells and whistles.

Think again about recent years. Can you be so sure?

What are we going to see when we reach the age of eighty? Ninety? One hundred? How will our lives be different if we do not adapt to technology. The ability to use technology to its fullest can and will impact your safety, your health, your relationships, the management of your time, your ability to stay current, and your ability to manage your finances. If you are reading this chapter and thinking, "Why should I care?" or that "These things are not necessary," consider this: Not knowing what we consider "advanced" functions today will guarantee illiteracy for the future. You can be sure that the impact of future technologies will have as much or more impact on our future lives as they have had in the past. They say getting older is not for cowards. Neither is it for the technologically shy! We do not want to pass on the learning of new technology to younger generations. To do so will make us dependent on others for our literacy. Whether we decide to embrace technology or not, the world will continue to evolve. We can choose to be left behind, or enjoy the benefits of advancing with the times.

They say getting older is not for cowards.
Neither is it for the technologically shy!

Technology enables your work, your pleasures, and your dreams.

Are you going to plug into technology or be left behind? We have been on a search for ways to learn technology and are embracing the changes. Once you have made the commitment to learn, you will want to take full advantage of the options. Mingle with youth. Connect with young people and you connect with technology. See what they are using and what technology they are discarding. Pay attention to the words you overhear.

Technology Quiz

Here is a quick quiz to see where you stand relative to today's technology. Let's see what technology you have mastered.

1. Yes No   Can you take a picture of your car with your cell phone and send it to your insurance agent?

2. Yes No   Can you get step-by-step driving directions audibly from your phone or car GPS system?

3. Yes No   Can you answer the phone in your car without touching your phone?

4. Yes No   Can you take a picture of your old curio chest, crop the picture to a smaller size, and upload it to an online auction site?

5. Yes No   Can you connect your laptop to a wide-screen TV to view the pictures taken on your last trip?

6. Yes No   Can you send a copy of your W-2s as a fax to your CPA by using only your phone, tablet, or PC?

7. Yes No   Can you monitor your heart rate, number of calories burned, and number of steps walked by using your smartphone?

8. Yes No   Can you deposit checks into your checking or savings account using your smart phone?

9. Yes No   Can you use a personal hot spot to connect to the Internet?

10. Yes No   Have you used a square? (Hint: It is used in credit card transactions.)

How did you do?
If you answered "Yes":

1-3 times: It is time to catch up on technology!

4-5 times: You have a good technology foundation.

7-8 times: You were considered advanced in the race to technology just a few years ago. But look over your shoulder, others are catching up fast!

9-10 times: Bravo! You are technologically current. Consider helping others along!

Learning Technology

So how do you learn? Here are a few of our favorite ways:

Option 1: *Internet resources*

YouTube is an excellent source. You can access it from your Internet browser by typing in YouTube. YouTube is a platform where individuals can produce their own videos. Many of these producers are college professors, technology experts, or users who spent hours learning how to do something and decided to share the information with you. For example, once you are at YouTube.com, type "depositing a check using your cell phone" in the search window. Several videos will appear giving instructions for this activity. YouTube videos are short, so you will want to watch several in order to get as much information as is available. We tested all of the capabilities in our technology quiz, so if you want to learn more, YouTube is a good start. However, we must warn you: Once you are learning in YouTube, you will be addicted.

Meetup.com is another great source. Meetup groups consist of people in your own neighborhood who share similar interests. You can simply type your interest into the search option in order to see if there is already a group dedicated to sharing their interests in learning more about technology. If there are no groups available, you can start a new group and see if anyone is interested in joining you. You get a double benefit for your efforts: You learn about technology, and you may meet new friends!

Option 2: *Go to the source*
Another favorite way of learning technology is to simply go to the store where they sell your device. As long as you are not in the store on a busy day or at a busy time, the customer service specialist would be happy to help you. Better yet, call first and set up an appointment with them, letting them know your area of need. By setting an appointment, you have given them the opportunity to prepare materials for you in advance. During our last purchase of cellular technology, we found that our cell phone provider offers a free class that included such topics as: linking your tablet with your phone, creating hot spots using your phone to share Internet connectivity with multiple devices, how to use Dropbox to store documents in the cloud and share these documents across your devices, and, of course, how to make a simple phone call. People in the classes come from all levels of experience. Having attended these classes, we can assure you that they are as patient with teaching people how to perform advanced functions as they are showing people how to turn the volume down.

Option 3: *Attend a class at your local college, senior center, or community center*
There may be a fee associated with these classes, but this approach is particularly helpful if you like

the step-by-step method or know that you need more formal instruction. Classes will often be supported with handouts, and will take on a more formal approach. Classes may take up to four hours and may include sections that cater to basic, intermediate, and advanced levels of skill. This will help you get into a group that best matches your own level.

Option 4: *Ask a young'un*

Young people are a treasure trove of technical knowledge and skills. However, the common complaints about young'uns are that they go too fast, do not explain, and tend to mumble. In order to circumvent this, recognize that teaching may be new to this person and that you—yes, you—are not their typical student. Explain that you are writing out instructions to "e-mail to a friend," so you need the correct terminology to explain the process as simply as possible. Depending on the age of your teacher, a plate of chocolate chip cookies or a beer might help. Choose wisely according to size and age. Remember, though, that this young'un is an expert and has been for years. You can prove this to yourself: Remember whom you asked to set the clock on your VHS recorder? The young'un you will want to ask is that person's son or daughter.

Now, does all this learning seem like you could have other options and return to a simpler life, become dependent on others, or avoid technology all together? Just keep reminding yourself that if you had stayed in a simpler life, you never would have a cell phone and you never would have recorded a movie. If everyone had avoided learning technology, you would have to wait two weeks for your medical records to arrive, you would not know how to get to your doctor's office if you had not been there before, you would not be able to pick up the results of your blood tests from your medical portal, and you would not be able to issue a question to your insurance company. If you stop now, who knows what you will not be able to do in twenty years. When was the last time you had film developed into prints? Point made.

We forgot to mention the most important reason why you need to stay current with technology: to stay productive in the work force.

Work and Financial Management

Choose a job you love and you will never have to work a day in your life.
—CONFUCIOUS

Work

Many baby boomers suffer from the effects of the Second Great Depression. Because of economic realities, combined with a propensity to save less than they would need for retirement, baby boomers are faced with a challenge: supporting thirty or more years of active living with an unknown and uncertain picture of their finances. For many baby boomers, the solution to this challenge is to continue working on a full- or part-time basis well into their seventies or eighties. Longer working careers mean that TAs need to find ways to merge pleasure, purpose, and work. In Act III—regardless of how you have viewed work—work now must equal purpose; purpose must equal pleasure.

In Act III—regardless of how you have viewed
work—work now must equal purpose; purpose
must equal pleasure.

TAs need to see work as a choice, a choice of making the best use of their time. This may require a single, sometimes difficult, shift in thinking. Work during our career-building years included competition, building savings to get somewhere (a house, a family, a series of awesome vacations, an adopted child), and fulfillment. Somewhere before or during Act III, we discover something fascinating about our work life: It is not so much what we do; it is how we do it.

We are reminded about the movie, *Mr. Holland's Opus*. In the movie, based on real life, Mr. Holland sacrifices his dream of writing the great American opus because he is distracted by the need to earn money for a newborn baby, deal with the medical costs of a deaf child, and pay for everyday needs of life. Instead of writing his opus, he teaches music to seemingly untalented children, instructs fifteen-year-olds how to drive, and deals with normal passions of family and relationships. In his eyes, he was a failure with a half-written manuscript. However, his manuscript was complete in a way he had not considered. At the end of the movie, we see the fruits of his labor—the performance of his opus by his students, successful in their own walks of life, due to his support, kindness, and dedication. His opus was not music, but his impact on others. What if we all knew our true impact on things that we think are routine, meaningless, and "work"?

What if we all knew our true impact
on things that we think are routine,
meaningless, and "work"?

In ACT III, we are selfish with our time, wanting to squeeze the maximum benefit out of it. We will not sacrifice our valuable time for false promises of promotion or uproot our homes, friendships, and stability to pursue opportunities. On the other hand, we thrive on enjoyable experiences. "Enjoyable" is defined differently by each of us. For one person, working a minimally paid job as a social worker in the inner city may provide the fulfillment that makes each day rewarding. For another, he or she may explore a forgotten craft. Others may have discovered the joy in their work many years ago and would not even consider leaving it. It is not only okay to continue working, it is highly recommended—if work can add purpose. What makes work more enjoyable? Many studies show the joy one finds in work has little to do with money.

Sometimes our internal programming says a job, to be real, has to be forty hours a week with benefits. This is not always true. By thinking out of the box, opportunities can materialize and offer exciting options.

After selling his business, Craig thought he never again would be employable. One day at the gym, a friend told him about a start-up company needing some general help that might include a little writing, prepping marketing materials, moving boxes around the office, and helping with seminars. Since the sale of his business had yielded less than expected, Craig thought that a small part-time job would fill the gap between his meager savings and his expenses.

As it turned out, the small writing tasks required that Craig learn how to do some simple web design and he was able to travel to seminar locations to take the pictures for the website. In these seminars, he met other people who asked him how much he would charge for similar tasks: writing small articles, taking pictures, and developing their websites. Soon Craig found that he did not have one job, he had five. Though he was working thirty-five to fifty hours a week, he worked according to his own time schedule. During the day, he and his wife could take tai chi lessons offered at the local community center. Uploading a few pictures before breakfast gave him the freedom to catch the matinees for new movie releases. Work no longer interfered with what he wanted to do. It was another activity in his self-defined life.

Craig created a working scenario in a way that matches our three requirements for successful Act III careers. In order for a TA to believe that work is a good use of his or her time, the work must be relevant, provide a reason to relate to others, and keep one current in today's skills. Let's explore this further.

Figure 3: Act III Work Circles

To be *relevant* means that the skills you offer are significant to others. Often, older workers fall into the trap of playing historian, remembering what went well in the past and lamenting that the ways of the past are fading. You will find them singing the mantra of "we used to do it in such and such a way." They are experts at this role, giving you all the names of people who were in charge ten years ago and remembering with the glassy eyes of fondness the glories of the old days. For a while, these historians can be valuable, but their value will fade quickly. Compare this to the role that Craig played. He was a scout. He was helping a start-up move forward. All ideas were fresh and untried. His skills, his knowledge, and his achievements were relevant.

Relatable means that the individual is involved in a give-and-take relationship with one's coworkers. As an Italian neighbor used to say, "One hand washes the other." Older workers will sometimes draw away from the main group, thinking that they are more experienced, knowledgeable, or mature. The tendency to draw away can be particularly strong if the culture of the company embraces a younger workforce. The decision not to relate can have dire results. Other people need to know what your skills are; they need you to understand theirs. They will want to take the lead sometimes and will expect you to support them. They will be more likely to ask you for your opinion if you ask them for theirs. You may not want to join in on the Friday karaoke night but if you did you might be surprised at the change in everyone's attitude toward you on Monday morning.

Currency is the third element of a successful Act III career. Craig learned how to develop a web page as a new skill in order to perform his job. He did not say, "I'm not into the new way," he embraced the opportunity to learn. Attending seminars and trade shows exposed him to new ideas and trends. No one looked at his age when he was guiding them in the requirements for web publishing!

If TAs concentrate on these three areas, they will find themselves feeling more appreciated and valued. New opportunities and projects will come their way along with learning opportunities and the chance to work with a variety of people. Work will take on a new feeling that may help the TAs decide that work is something they will want to do for just a little longer. Work can become a choice.

Your Act III Career

Think about the work that you perform as an employee, volunteer, or member of your community. Determine what aspects of the job are relevant, relatable, and current. Is there something that you want to change in that activity or the way you relate to others? How can you update your skills?

Are you RELEVANT?

List activities that you are involved in.	How relevant is it?	What can be done to make it more relevant or can the activity be passed to someone else?

Are you RELATABLE?

List activities that you are involved in.	Do you do these alone or with others?	How can you engage others in this work?
List activities that others do that affect you.	To what extent are you involved in this activity?	How can you engage with others in this work?
List something that you would like someone to help you with.	Who might help you with this activity?	
What skills can your offer others?	Who might be helped with this skill?	

Are you CURRENT?

What skills do you use that demonstrate current skills?	What activities do you NOT perform because you "don't know how"?	Is this a skill that you could learn or improve?

Now, review the activities you have just listed. Under each area of the Work Circles, write three changes that you can identify that could make your contribution more relevant, relatable, and current.

Act III Work Circles

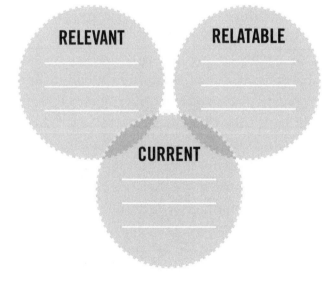

Financial Management
The Act III Financial Challenge

We often find that people's interests and dreams are simply blocked by their perception of financial reality. During tax time, many come into Paula's office and in the course of the interview, make statements like, "I wish I could retire, but I cannot afford to" or "I'd love to travel more, but . . ." These statements often are untrue but believed. James was a successful horticulturalist working part time for two local botanical gardens and his wife, Kathy, helped him with some of his office work. They agreed to take the three-part Act III Financial Challenge that would enable them to view their current spending and get an accurate picture of what their financial resources would be if they chose to stop working. When you read their story and see their financial numbers, know that your numbers will be different but the process will be the same. Like James and Kathy, you will find opportunities to substitute, replace, sell, or gather in order to make the adjustments you need to transition your finances into Act III.

James and Kathy enjoyed an after-tax income of $8,487 a month. For Part I of the Act III Financial Challenge, they tracked their daily spending for one month. The results of their tracking are summarized in *Exercise Example 3*. Please note that you can use your own methods of tracking but we have provided our Act III Financial Challenge Forms at www.myact3.com.

Exercise Example 3: Act III Financial Challenge:
PART I: EXPENSE BASELINE

Expense Baseline

Food and Beverage	$	700
Transportation		294
Residence		2,000
Entertainment		450
Entertaining		200
Travel and Vacation		300
Household		400
Technology		300
Clothes		240
Self-Indulgence		500
Pets		500
Other Family Members		1,000
Memberships and Charities		-
Healthcare		150
Health Insurance		702
Expense Baseline	$	7,736

After-tax Income	$	8,487
Expense Baseline		7,736
Money left over at end of month	$	751

James and Kathy could not see how they could quit their jobs with $751 left over each month. Nonetheless, they returned to Paula's office to take Part II of the challenge. This component encouraged them to take a hard look at their expenses and examine how small or large adjustments could be made to their overall spending.

Exercise Example 4: Act III Financial Challenge:
PART II: ADJUSTING MONTHLY EXPENSES

	Baseline	Savings	New Baseline
Food and Beverage	$ 700	$ 400	$ 300
Transportation	294	210	84
Residence	2,000		2,000
Entertainment	450	250	200
Entertaining	200	100	100
Travel and Vacation	300		300
Household	400		400
Technology	300		300
Clothes	240	140	100
Self-Indulgence	500	300	200
Pets	500		500
Other Family Members	1,000	800	200
Memberships and Charities	-		-
Healthcare	150		150
Health Insurance	702		702
Total Expense	$ 7,736	$ 2,200	$ 5,536

Savings Strategies

James and Kathy experimented with changes they thought they could manage in order to see if their financial picture could improve. They were amazed at how easily they identified changes that could save them $2,200 a month. Once they got into the habit of evaluating their spending, they found new ways of finding value in their day-to-day living. They mindfully changed their spending habits in several ways. For example:

Food and Beverage: Instead of going to a restaurant for lunch, they purchased several nice containers to keep salads cold and soups warm. Kathy began making inexpensive soups that were legume based. So instead of spending $8-$12 each for a café lunch, she and James enjoyed a bowl of homemade minestrone and crusty bread. Because they preplanned their meals, they had an extra bonus. James lost twenty pounds and Kathy twelve, effortlessly. Savings from Food and Beverage: $400.

Transportation: Instead of driving both cars daily, they made their transportation into a game. They made bets on how long one of their cars could stay in the garage during the month. Neither wanted to lose their playful bet so they started to share rides using the car that had better gas mileage, started to combine trips, and began to enjoy their time at home more. Savings from Transportation: $210.

Entertainment and Entertaining: Instead of going out each weekend with friends, they instituted a "Movie

Night with James and Kathy." They would choose a video to watch and supplied gourmet popcorn and snacks for their guests. They grew closer to their friends who now come to dinner in their shorts and they all converse without feeling that it is time to leave their restaurant table. They discovered free summer concerts, library lectures, and Internet television. Premium cable channels were substituted by dollar-a-night rental DVDs. Instead of having breakfast at a waterfront restaurant, they enjoyed a Sunday brunch picnic by the lake—like they used to enjoy when courting. Savings from Entertainment: $250. Savings from Entertaining: $100.

Clothes: They discovered an outlet shop to replace the mall. Since they were entertaining at home and exploring casual entertaining options, they were wearing casual clothes more. Their dry cleaning bills were reduced to almost nothing. They purchased their clothes off-season and tried to curb their impulsive buying habit. Savings from Clothes: $140.

Self-Indulgence: Throughout their lives, James and Kathy loved boating. They decided to pass down their beloved boat to their son and split the costs of docking and maintenance. This saved them hundreds and the boat is now getting more use than ever. Savings from Self-Indulgence: $300.

Other Family Members: James and Kathy had been providing financial support when their adult children would run into a cash need or when they wanted to simply shower them with "love." They had a conversation with each to explain that they were trying to stay within a budget that would support them through their lifestyle change into their Act III. They let each know that if they truly needed their financial support, they would do everything they could to help them when the situation arose. Savings from Other Family Members: $800.

James and Kathy made all these changes to their spending habits. But before they took the plunge of quitting their jobs, they came back to the office to get Part III of the Act III Financial Challenge: Change to Income. This part allowed them to consider what money would be coming to them in the future.

While working through Part III, they listed out the financial impact of quitting their three W-2 jobs replacing that income with their social security benefits. They kept the small interest, dividends, and estimated tax refunds (calculated as a monthly amount). James and Kathy also planned on getting small pensions of $900, $700, and $200 a month from companies they worked for. To get an accurate estimate of their social security benefits, they visited the Social Security Retirement Estimator at http:// www.ssa.gov/retire2/estimator.htm. By answering a few simple questions, they received an immediate answer on the amount they would receive monthly if they were to retire during the next twelve months. The following is their result from Part III.

Exercise Example 5: Act III Financial Challenge:
PART III: CHANGE TO INCOME

	BASELINE	TRANSITION TO ACT III
James's Job	$2,700	$
James's 2nd Job	2,400	
Kathy's Job	3,000	
James's Pension		900
James's 2nd Pension		700
Kathy's Pension		200
James's Social Security		2,585
Kathy's Social Security		1,960
Interest	100	100
Dividends	120	120
Estimated Tax Refund (divided by 12)	167	167
Total Income	$8,487	$ 6,732

	BASELINE	NEW BASELINE	ACT III CHANGES
After-tax Income	$8,487	$ 6,732	$ 1,755
Less: Expenses	7,736	5,536	2,200
Money Left over at end of Month	$ 751	$ 1,196	$ 445

Their income dropped from $8,487 a month to $6,732 by replacing their earned income with social security benefits and pensions, a decrease of $1,755 a month. But remember, their living expenses dropped by $2,200 a month leaving them with $1,196 left over for emergencies and planned splurges.

After getting a clear vision of their financial picture, they immediately called the office demanding an appointment. They came in to deliver a bottle of champagne to celebrate their decision to quit their jobs and transition from earned income to three small pensions and social security benefits. They could not believe that they lived in fear of the future for years when all it took was a dedicated effort to face the realities of choices in lifestyle.

Summary

Before continuing to Section 5 of this book, take a few minutes to reflect on your technology goals, relevancy goals, relatable goals, currency goals, and financial goals.

In the area below, list your "top three." You will be using these in the last section.

Technology Goals

1._____

2._____

3._____

Relevancy Goals

1._____

2._____

3._____

Relatable Goals

1._____

2._____

3._____

Currency Goals

1._____

2._____

3._____

Financial Goals

1._____

2._____

3._____

Health

If I'd known I was going to live this long,
I'd have taken better care of myself.
—EUBIE BLAKE

HEALTH HAS ALWAYS BEEN an important part of living out our dreams. In childhood, developmental issues could hold us back from learning or interacting with others. Good health could support our ability to play in sports or enable us to impress our friends with the city's longest handstand. Teenagers may be more prone to accidents and need to balance their maturing bodies with their desires to live out dauntless adventures. Young-adult life is filled with setbacks due to pregnancy, back injuries, and overindulgence in recreational libations. At the same time, young adults are at the highest level of conditioning, supporting the long days of multitasking, raising a family, and working those extra hours to get enough for the down payment on a new home. Our bodies and our goals are connected. So as we enter Act III, our health issues are not necessarily worse, but they may be different.

Our bodies and our goals are connected.

Recent articles address the five, eight, or ten top health issues for older folks. The lists will vary in detail, but here are the most frequently mentioned, in alphabetical order:

Arthritis
Cancer
Depression
Diabetes
Gastrointestinal Issues
Hearing Impairment
Heart Disease
High Blood Pressure
Osteoporosis
Respiratory Problems
Sleep Disorder
Thyroid
Ulcers
Urinary Disorders
Visual Disorders
Weight Management

Well, that looks pretty impressive, doesn't it? But not everyone suffers from these issues, and certainly not all of them. While most of the diseases listed take time to develop, they are not *caused* by getting older. Some unfortunate TAs may look at a diagnosis and pronounce, "Well, there it is, this is the one that got me. Yup, Mom had the same thing." In many ways, the disease becomes a self-fulfilling prophesy: because the disease is "expected," one does little to slow down the disease's onset or progression. Unfortunately, it may be the way your doctor looks at it, too. If a thirty-year-old goes to a physician and complains of a sore knee, the first question will be, "How did you hurt it?" When a TA goes into the office with the same issue, the question will more likely be, "What medications have you been taking for it?" In the first case, the sore knee was seen as an exception so the goal was to diagnose the situation and get the person back to health. In the second situation, the assumption was made that the sore knee was the result of age and little could be done to resolve the issue. As TAs, our objective should be to obtain and maintain our best level of health rather than handling sickness.

As TAs, our objective should be to obtain
and maintain our best level of health
rather than handling sickness.

Most of us know that we can do a better job of taking care of our health. In the last fifty to sixty years, life expectancy has been increased not only by advancements in medicine, but also by behavioral and environmental improvements. Fortunately, there are some easy steps we can take to avoid the diseases we mentioned above. The steps start with establishing our baselines. After examining your baselines, you will find that there is not one magical path to good health, but a combination of approaches that lead to overall mental and physical well-being.

So, let's start by taking a look at our baselines, beginning with medical tests.

Figure 4: Act III Target Areas of Health

Baseline Medical Tests

Baseline tests are like markers that help you track whether or not your key indicators of health are changing. Since no test has a best number for everyone, it is far more useful to spot a change or trend than it is to get a one-time reading. Your primary health-care professional will help you identify other baselines based on your personal or family history, but the following are the most common:

Medical Tests
Baseline Medical Test Tracker

Baseline Medical Tests	Last Test Date	Need to Schedule
Blood Pressure		
Blood Sugar		
Bone Density Scan		
Cholesterol Profile		
Dental Exam		
Eye Exam/Glaucoma Screen		
Rectal Health Exam		
Skin Check		
Sleep Study		
Thyroid Test		

The information you share with your doctor, including goals and concerns, will help direct your plan of health, not just your plan of care. Do not fall into the trap of assuming that all health problems are the result of age.

Talk with your primary health physician about your goal of having your Act III be as healthy and active as possible. If you have a good relationship with your doctor, then this conversation will be an easy one for both of you. If you feel at all uncomfortable, put it in writing: Write down your list of concerns, your desire to have your Act III be as healthy and active as possible, and your questions. Give the list to your doctor and make the conversation happen. Remember, the information you share with your doctor, including goals and concerns, will help direct your plan of health, not just your plan of care. Do not fall into the trap of assuming that all health problems are the result of age. If you have multiple doctors or practitioners that you are seeing for different health issues, make sure your primary care physician is aware of their plan of care and medications. If your doctors order appropriate tests, don't just accept a simple readout. Make sure that your primary care physician has a copy of all tests because he or she will likely be the only one who sees the "big picture" of your health. Schedule an appointment with your specialists and primary care physician to review the results of any tests and discuss what can be done. Physicians like to work with patients who are committed to their health and when they see that you are putting forth an effort (and following through with advice) doctors tend to go the extra mile for you.

Strength and Balance

It is important for you to consult with a personal trainer or physical therapist knowledgeable in the changing dynamics of the aging body. Whereas a twenty-year-old might be concerned with getting a six-pack, your concern may be stronger ankles, better balance, or a stronger core. Some may need to reach their goals while adapting to restrictions. Strength exercises help maintain muscle mass which can decrease naturally as we age—up to a pound per year. Those who have not been active should not begin training for a marathon that is scheduled just a month away. A better choice is to start by strengthening trunk, arms, and leg muscles. Stretching exercises are often overlooked, yet they increase range of motion, joint flexibility, and reduce the chance of injury. Strengthening muscles, tendons, and ligaments around joints can reduce joint pain.

Food Selections

Back in high school, you may have learned that humans are made up of forty-six chromosomes. These chromosomes, in turn, are made up of DNA patterns called genes. The genes function as sets of instructions that determine whether or not we will be short or tall, have blue eyes or brown eyes, or have the propensity to develop gallstones when we reach the age of forty. Sure, we could do things that might help, but basically, we believed that we were hardwired to live out the edict of those genes.

Enter the world of epigenetics, the science that explores how our genes are affected by our environment, diet, and emotions. As it turns out, there is more intelligence at the level of the cell than we thought. It is true that DNA determines what we are, but DNA must make a copy of itself in order rebuild cells. According to the theory, RNA, the copy agent of DNA, organizes itself by copying the blueprint instructions of the DNA. However, we are now finding out that RNA is not always the obedient follower of those instructions. The fact that RNA can be more flexible allows cells to react to the environment. In *Food for Thought: An Epigenetic Guide to Wellness*, authors George Febish and Jo Anne Oxley likened the intelligence of the cell to a software program that can turn on or turn off certain genes from expressing themselves. This intelligence is critical, since our cells contain from thirty thousand to forty thousand genes, all with different instructions on how your body should look and function.

So, it appears that, while there are some hardwired instructions, each cell must use its own memory and intelligence in making decisions about which genes will be turned on or off. Some old genes are hanging around the cells that are no longer useful. If these genes were to be turned on, it might be detrimental. A tumor, for example, might develop if a certain gene were to be turned on, or if the "inhibitor" gene failed to turn on.

At the same time, our genes live in a food environment that is changing rapidly. In our youth, food came from the local farmer and fast food meant a sandwich or leftovers from the fridge. Children carried lunch bags and families packed picnic baskets for the road. But as we grew into our teenage years, we were more likely to find a quick meal at a fast-food chain or calm our hunger pangs with chips from a vending machine. Microwaves came into the picture offering quick and processed solutions, and genetically modified fruits and vegetables entered the marketplace to respond to our needs to produce food faster and cheaper.

The way our food is being produced has also changed dramatically. Livestock are fed nutrients, hormones, and antibiotics that carry into the foods that we eat. Pesticides make sure our foods are insect-free, and preservatives are added to ensure that the food transported from Chile to New York looks good in the supermarket. The problem is, at the cell level, how do our cells react to all of these changes? There has not been enough time for the hardwiring to adjust. The cell doesn't just need "good food," it needs food that will help it make the right decisions. How is the cell to deal with all of the changes it has been dealt? How can we help that poor little cell?

The cell doesn't just need "good food," it needs
food that will help it make the right decisions.

We can take steps to better our nutrition, keep our
emotions supportive, and reduce toxins. You do not
have time NOT to learn more about nutrition since
nutrition can act as a natural physician. Consider
the following discoveries. Allium vegetables, such
as garlic, inhibit the growth of breast-cancer cells.
Broccoli and other cruciferous vegetables may ward
off cancer by turning on genes that help destroy car-
cinogens. Other elements may assist in telling the
cell to suppress tumor growth. Chard can help reg-
ulate blood sugar, improve circulation, rebuild bone,
improve your hair, and contribute to eye health. It is
time that you learned more about the health powers
of food and took them seriously!

Chances are, the last time you went to see the doctor,
he or she made a comment that had something to
do with food. Perhaps you were cautiously advised
to drop twenty pounds. Perhaps it was suggested
that you cut down on foods that might contribute to
cholesterol or you were told to eat smaller meals and
cut back on sugar. The next time the conversation
heads in this direction, we would advise that instead
of rolling your eyes or shaking the comment off with,
"Yeah, yeah, I know," you change your approach.
Tell your doctor that you think it would be a great
idea and you would like a referral to a dietitian or

nutritionist; then explain that you would really like to maximize your health plan with appropriate bio-active foods. After your doctor recovers from the shock, he or she will likely supply information and contacts that will help you explore new ways of controlling your health.

Immunizations

We are not medically trained but we have learned some things about our own health and desire for good health. Your doctor will have recommendations on immunizations for you; discuss these and then give the permission for the ones you choose. Currently, the Center for Disease Control recommends that seniors obtain the following vaccinations: influenza, Tdap (tetanus, diphtheria, whooping cough), shingles, and pneumonia (PPSV23).

Attitudes and Emotions

Attitudes and emotions are significant determinants of our health. How often do you smile? How would you describe your smile? Is it sincere and from your heart? Is it a social mask or a cover for anger? Different smile types will have different physiological impacts on brain chemistry. Many studies show that heartfelt smiles release endorphins, the body's natural painkiller. Smiling makes us feel relaxed and less stressed. So why don't we smile more?

Well, similar to the way our food supply has changed, our living environment has changed as well, creating more stress at our very core—our cells. Some people may argue that the world has not changed that much and that there has always been stress. Let's think about that one for a while.

Similar to the way our food supply has changed,
our living environment has changed as well,
creating more stress at our very core—our cells.

A few centuries back, the cell needed to deal with the "stress" of potential starvation, but that was not every year. Today our emotions must deal with complex and remote family structures, multiple jobs, multitasking, increased work demands, changing roles, increasing diversity, competition and monitoring. Imagine life in 1950. You could pretty much count on a workweek limited to forty hours. If you had to travel for work, you had a "travel day" where you were not expected to produce work (after all, you were away from your typewriter). You didn't have to answer text messages— someone was answering the call back at the office. When you called to check on your flight, a travel agency made the arrangements. In any event, you had been on the job for twenty years, so people knew you would take care of things when you came back.

What happened? Today that same worker needs to go online to arrange for the ticket and confirm the flight twenty-four hours before takeoff. Before getting on the plane, he or she must arrive an extra hour early to get through security checks. Meanwhile, a text comes in informing our worker that changes have been made in the PowerPoint and the new copy must be accessed before getting on the plane. A technical problem occurs. No problem, call tech support.

"Please press four for technical assistance; if you are calling about software, press one; for hardware issues press two; for other problems press three."

"Please enter the five-digit code associated with your computer." "Please enter your user pass code." "I'm sorry, you have entered the wrong pass code." "I am sorry you are having trouble. Please check the pass code and call back."

"Grrrrr." Can you see why we deal with more emotions?

There are many techniques to help reduce stress. You might note some of the most common to add to your plan for Act III health.

- Spend time gardening
- Spend time with a pet
- Get a massage
- Get a pedicure
- Call a friend you haven't talked to for a while
- Have a simple sit-down dinner
- Turn on calming music
- Watch a good comedy and have a good laugh
- Exercise
- Engage in a hobby
- Read a good book

It is important to set aside at least half an hour a day to do something enjoyable for yourself. Remember that, with so many stressors, taking time to reduce stress is as important as any act of hygiene. In Act III, we invite you to pursue those interests that give you the greatest joy. In our various keep, toss, add exercises, we reduce stressors and align with our desires. Food choice and exercise changes help reduce stress. By saying "I choose," you assure that you are selecting options consciously. In a future section of this book called "Nurturing Your Soul," you will learn to practice reconnecting with your soul.

Physical Activity

Once you have made the commitment of being physically active in your Act III, the question now is, "What activity?"

It is important to know your baseline activity level: Perhaps the most effective way of obtaining your baseline activity level is to simply purchase a pedometer that measures the number of steps you take in a given period of time. Cecilia purchased a wrist pedometer and used a setting that allowed her to capture the number of steps, rather than miles, taken in a day. A few months later, Paula discovered that her new smartphone came with an app that did the same thing—including a measure of her heart rate.

At the time of our baseline measures, both of us were working in academia and experienced what one might call a sedentary lifestyle. It was a little more than that. Since we both had administrative and teaching responsibilities, and worked in private accounting and analytics businesses, we tended to work twelve-hour days, sitting in a padded chair. We treated our bodies like tripods for our brains. We took our brains for a drive to the office, walked our brains into the office, walked our brains to the mail room, took a restroom break, and refreshed our coffee cups. In the evening we carried our brains into the classroom, where we got a little more exercise walking around the room as we lectured.

We treated our bodies like
tripods for our brains.

Our first readings on the pedometer added up to a whopping 2,500 steps—not quite ready for a marathon. However, weekends were a different story. Cecilia, an avid gardener, would then boost her activity level to 15,000 steps on the weekends. She would haul gardening soil, rake leaves, rearrange garden furniture, and spread mulching compost from early morning to evening, leaving only enough time to pack her sore muscles in ice and grab the aspirin bottle for relief. Not a good spread of exercise.

Paula, on the other hand, had been in the emergency room twice in the previous twelve months for arthritis of the knee, barely able to stand. During the weekends, she would give her knee tender recuperating care and her pedometer reading was reduced as a result. This was also less than an ideal program. So what did we do about it? Well, at first, we said, "We need to start going to the gym and working out." Then we stayed silent for a while, looked at each other, and in one voice shouted, "You've got to be kidding!" Then we thought of a technique we often used with clients who were resisting change: Find the smallest possible thing you can do to make an improvement and start with that.

Then we thought of a technique we often used with clients who were resisting change: Find the smallest possible thing you can do to make an improvement and start with that.

Creating a Health Plan

The technique we used with our clients is called Kaizen. Perhaps you have used this method in work improvement groups. Kaizen philosophy believes that large changes are met with resistance. Just think about the last time you set an impressive New Year's resolution. Probably didn't last long, right? The human psyche resists change. After all, your entire body, mind, and soul have been put into balance just to keep the delicate equilibrium that allows you to sleep at a certain hour, get up on time, eat the right amount of food, and find a way to survive in a world that asks you to make a living, raise children, volunteer, keep up a clean house and yard, and not wear the same shirt two days in a row. Change? Well, why? What does it mean to the delicate balance? Soon, your impressive resolution is cancelled and balance is no longer in threat.

Kaizen solves this resistance by asking, "What small thing can I do that will make a difference in this situation?" The very question sounds safe and nonthreatening. What's more, the question sets the mind into a quest for information. Rather than offering resistance, the mind looks for solutions and finds satisfaction in finding (and helping to implement) the ideas that surface.

Imagine that you wanted to take a vacation in Costa Rica and discovered that the trip had a five thousand dollar price tag. You check your bank account against the price tag and decide there is no way you can afford the splurge. Then you change the question to "What small thing can I do today to make this vacation a possibility?" Suddenly, you notice that old guitar sitting in your garage and put it on eBay. When was the last time you played that—1992? The next day you ask yourself the same question and remember that you had placed that old gold jewelry in a cardboard box and stuck it in the back of the closet for a rainy day. Bet it rains in Costa Rica! Ask the question again, and you discover a part-time pet-sitting job, a way to save on a cable bill, or a plan to entertain at home as an alternative to a restaurant gathering. In an amazing period of time, the five thousand dollars is in your hand not because of anything dramatic, but because you uncovered the secret of taking the first small step.

Using this philosophy to build our personal health plan intrigued us. We thought we could improve our health doing the "small things" approach rather than attempting a grand overhaul. We developed our physical activity plans following our Toss-Hold-Add approach.

Exercise Example 6: Act III Physical Activity Plan

Cecilia's Physical Activity Plan

Toss	Hold	Add
Limit weekend activity to 8,000 steps a day max.	Maintain 2,500 steps currently at work.	Add 1,000 steps daily by doing a small amount of yard work every morning.
Sell bicycle since it won't be used.		Sit on balance ball thirty minutes a day to strengthen core—can be done while doing normal work.
	Follow up with plan in two months.	Consult with personal trainer for low-impact exercises to do at desk.

Paula's Physical Activity Plan

Toss	Hold	Add
	Talk with physical therapist to see what safe activities can be done without further injury to knee.	
	Maintain 2,000 steps currently at work.	Work on upper-body strength by using hand weights while watching Dr. Who reruns.
		Buy a video on chair yoga.
	Follow up with plan in two months.	

Now it is your time to work on your Act III Physical
Activity Plan.

My Act III Physical Activity Plan

Toss	Hold	Add

Relationships

...When you learn to live for others,
they will live for you.
—PARAMAHANSA YOGANANDA

A SAN DIEGO RADIO SHOW recently asked people what they would do if they had one extra hour a day. The most common answer: Spend that hour with family! According to a survey conducted by the National Council on Aging and *USA Today*, the concern over one's relationships with family and friends (40%) topped financial concerns (30%).

The challenge TAs have with relationships is that the development of new relationships grows more difficult and current relationships will change. How you look at these changing relationships will determine if you have a list of excuses or bushel of opportunities.

During Act III, the characters in your life's play will adjust,
as they have in every major stage of your life.

During Act III, the characters in your life's play will adjust, as they have in every major stage of your life. Your children have grown up, married, and perhaps relocated. Your coworkers have been promoted, downsized, or retired and moved on. You may have moved away from the workforce. Parents often have friends related to their child's activities—PTA, band parents, football boosters, soccer moms. Relationships built upon these activities will fade away. Friends and relatives may have left your relationship circle due to divorce, relocation, poor health, or death. It is time for a choice. TAs can choose to recast their life's play so that it is compatible with a life that looks forward, a life that is supported, and a life that is positive and full.

Review the Excuses, the Hurts, and the Limitations

Where do you harbor a belief that you are or were under someone else's control? Forgive the limitations other's had. Forgive the fact that you didn't know then what you know now. Consider Paul's story.

Paul's mother died when he was young and he was raised by a single father. He was the middle of five children, all boys. He received little attention from his older brothers whose limited caregiving skills were reserved for the younger brothers. Paul was responsible for the household where his chores included dusting, preparing light meals, and vacuuming.

Fortunately, Paul loved to read and reading was his escape. He did well in school but tended to rebel against authority. In many ways he was beyond his years, facing more responsibilities than most children his age. He felt that because of his adult roles, he was entitled to critique his teachers. He was also somewhat outspoken as to what classroom requirements he would or would not do. Since he liked weight lifting, he tried to bond with older boys and men at the gym by using what he considered to be manly phrases (curse words). His new language blended with his outspoken manner. When teachers tried to correct him, he interpreted their action as being disrespectful of his intellect and his value.

After three years of college, Paul quit because he was "smarter than the professors." On the job, he found that corporate America undervalued his skills. Blinded by his own self-perception, Paul failed to realize that, in spite of the hardships he had experienced, he was the cause of many of his problems. Employers shied away from hiring and promoting someone whose conversation was sprinkled with colorful and inappropriate language. When he left a room, people would exhale and just shake their heads. This was unfortunate because under his toughened crust, Paul was a hard worker and tried to help people in any way that he could. He had a huge heart.

Paul felt that other people were holding him back. Perhaps he had studied the wrong thing? Perhaps he had entered the wrong career? Paul is in his fifties now, bemoaning the fact that he cannot get more than basic technical jobs. He feels that companies are just continuing to torment him with continuing signs of disrespect.

Paul is angry.

The truth is, Paul had more education than most people. He is well-read, and with a slight shift in attitude, would be a favorite candidate for any of the jobs he is interested in. But Paul has carried all the hurt and anger of childhood forward into his adult life. The anger he felt on behalf of the little motherless boy belonged to another age and another time. As he matured, the anger prevented him from expressing the attitude and interpersonal skills that he needed for his adult life. If Paul cannot adjust his attitude, his Act III will be just as gloomy.

Any unresolved issues from childhood and adulthood continue into Act III. They do not resolve themselves. Paul needed to face the issues that had haunted him all his life. He, and anyone like him, needs to act now!

We all have memories and beliefs that may interfere with our relationships. For example, what about the time your cousin had a party at the family lake house and didn't invite you. Let's see, it has been thirty years since you last talked with him? Bet he has forgotten all about it. Some people may feel that they are too old for a therapist and that professional help will not be valuable to them at this stage of life. However, TAs have the life skills of being able to reflect upon their lives with greater understanding and maturity. A few sessions with a therapist may help you sort out some nagging thoughts and help you embrace relationships more fully.

TAs cannot afford to deal with false limitations. What is the flaw that you don't think you need to deal with? What limits do you believe you have?

TAs cannot afford to deal with false limitations.
What is the flaw that you don't think you need to deal with?
What limits do you believe you have?

Evaluate Your Relationships

We encourage you to reach out now and start evaluating the actors in your current Act, and develop a casting call for the actors you will need moving forward. It is important to realize the difference between a character in your play and the extras that help set the scene. The extras are your acquaintances that you occasionally greet or interact with for short periods of time.

It is important to realize the difference between a character in your play and the extras that help set the scene.

Let us begin by evaluating the current players.

What you should consider when casting your characters:

1. Do you look forward to spending time with them? Or, do you feel depressed after being with them?
2. If you needed someone to pick you up at the airport or if your car ran out of gasoline, would you call this person?
3. Can you share your life's dreams with this person? Or, do your conversations stay at the surface level?
4. Does this person in some way support your interests, goals, or lifestyle?
5. Does this person bring in new insights or perspectives into your life?
6. Is this person someone you need to establish a relationship with for work, church, or school events, etc.?
7. Was this person once meaningful in your life but you have gone separate ways?

The following activity will help you reconsider the relationships in your Act III. List all your actors in the first column of your blank "Act III Relationship Grid." For each name on your list, ask yourself the questions listed above. This is an important step, so take your time. Reflect. Evaluate. Choose. For each name, decide whether you will keep that relationship, recast it into a new role, or sidestep the relationship.

The following grid shows an example of a shortened Act III Relationship Grid.

Exercise Example 7: Act III Relationship Grid

Name	Keep without change	Recast	Sidestep
Louise		Newly retired. Change from coworker to friend.	
Andrew	Very nurturing and with multiple interests in common.		
Lee	Spouse and soul mate.		
Brian			Negative attitude. Old reason for connection no longer valid. Not supportive.
Kaite	Positive attitude. Enjoys a variety of interests and is easy to blend with other friends.		
Mike		Neighbor. Always there in a pinch. Develop friendship to a deeper level.	
Aunt Julia	Keep. Last relative on Dad's side. While somewhat cranky, she is an important member and matriarch of the family.		

We hope your list is longer than this, but you get the idea. For the time being, imagine that this is your list. There may be some relationships that are perfect the way they are; but recognizing why the relationship works will help as you form new connections.

As you look at other players in your life you will see, as in the case of Brian, that the relationship was based on scenarios that have ended and, with no common interest going forward, the friendship is now obsolete. In other cases, as with Louise, the relationship must be adjusted because the scene has changed. The fact that Louise has retired and is no longer at the job where she can automatically connect for lunch and conversation means that you will need to make a concerted effort to find ways to arrange time together. Now, you can find new opportunities to build on the friendship outside of work. Fortunately, you and Louise anticipated the change, and for the last two years, have been exploring common interests outside of work—attending plays, sharing books, taking short overnight trips. As for Aunt Julia, the other alternatives for the relationship are not acceptable, so she remains in the "Keep" column.

Now, let's begin to evaluate your own list of connections and see how you want to deal with them as you cast your characters for your Act III. Remember that you want only those who will contribute positively to the life you choose to live.

My Act III Relationship Grid:

Name	Keep without change	Recast	Sidestep

Finding New Cast Members

Now that you have the names of the people who will be accompanying you into your Act III, it is time to consider new players who will enhance the quality of your story line. At this stage it is important to introduce diversity. Diversity is important because you may have limited your characters to those who mirrored your previous life roles. Now that your life is not based on the roles of "parent," "employee," or perhaps not even "spouse," you are freer in selecting people outside these spheres. If you are single, consider building more relationships with married couples, if you are married, consider adding a single person to your guest list. If you tend to mingle with people of the same age group, consider an event that mixes generations. If most of your friends are parents of your children's friends, consider joining organizations that will introduce people of different interests.

Consider all new sources for acquaintances and friends. Return to your mind map and consider organizations that support each circle of interest. To find these organizations, you might try the website Meetup.com that lists interest groups for your specific area. If your interest is not represented, you can start your own group. Another good source is various types of classes offered through local community centers and colleges. The advantage of these classes is that you have already defined a common interest before you join. Many associations such as the Orchid Society or sporting clubs will have open meetings that you can attend. If you attend an association meeting, try to get on a subcommittee so that you can be actively engaged with a smaller group. Many people look to volunteering opportunities. Make sure that you are truly interested in the cause these organizations represent. Try to find organizations where you will see people on a repeat basis or do an activity that is pleasurable. For example, Tim has always loved theater so he volunteers as an usher. As a benefit of helping people enjoy the evening, Tim is able to see first-run plays and has developed friendships with other ushers. These ushers have a common interest and can share memories of plays they have seen together. The organization gives them other opportunities to become involved, such as giving feedback on new plays or helping to select plays for the upcoming season. Sue volunteers at a resale shop for the local children's hospital, where she sees many people returning to the shop on a weekly and monthly basis. The repeat nature of the store's customers gives her a chance to connect with people in the community.

Consider working for a nonprofit organization. Many times, these organizations are looking for experienced people who are willing to work on a part-time or limited basis. While the pay may not be as high as for-profits, they offer a rewarding way to share one's talents, make a difference to the community, and associate with others of common interest.

Youth organizations offer an interesting way to connect with younger people and their parents. Becoming involved with these organizations may help you find younger acquaintances and friends as well as people in your own age group. You will be exposed to new ideas, and may become the "older friend" that you so cherished as a teenager.

Summary
Before continuing on in this book, take a few minutes to reflect on your health and relationship goals.

In the area below, list your "top three." You will be using these in the last section.

Health Test Goals:

1._____

2._____

3._____

Strength and Balance:

1._____

2._____

3._____

Food Choice Goals:

1._____

2._____

3._____

Immunization Goals:

1._____

2._____

3._____

Attitude Goals:

1._____

2._____

3._____

Physical Activity Goals:

1._____

2._____

3._____

Relationship Goals:

1._____

2._____

3._____

Nurturing Your Soul

If you realized how powerful your thoughts are,
you would never think a negative thought.
—PEACE PILGRIM

MANY CONFUSE NURTURING YOUR SOUL with pampering your body. Don't get us wrong, it is absolutely important to treat yourself to good chocolate, to take a bubble bath, or to pop open a cold brewski. These treats make you feel good or connect you to good memories of past experiences. When we were conducting our interviews, many said they were looking forward to the day when their lives could be filled with things they found pleasurable. This idea of pampering was more akin to what they had in mind—at least, in the beginning.

Nurturing, in contrast, is mindful encouragement of growth or development. So while the "chocolate" of life may soothe the soul, it does not nurture it.

How do you know if you are nurturing your soul? The signs are that you feel your own wisdom, you are naturally creative, you are at peace with who you are, and you are at peace with who others are. You feel connected to the person who just cut in front of you in line knowing that, at that moment, he somehow needed to be there.

If you are nurturing your soul, you realize that everything in your life fits together in a way that is seemingly miraculous. You feel free of restrictions, you are free from the fear of what others may think, and you have forgiven yourself for what you have and have not done. A nurtured soul is at peace with themselves and with others. It is inspired and ready for action.

Give Yourself Permission to Play

Who we are is not physical. Many philosophers, psychologists, and spiritual writers have tried to put a name to the self-observer who observes our thoughts and remembers our past. We will call it by two names: our soul and our spirit. Our soul is the accumulation of all our experiences with the ability to trigger the emotions tied to the specific ages of those experiences. Under the direction of your soul, you experience all the ages of your life. Bite into a chocolate chip cookie and you are four years old again—happy, content, and secure. Hear an adult yelling at a child and you become that third grader; your stomach churns as you feel your anger caused by the teacher who embarrassed you in front of the class and made you stand in the corner for a time-out. See a good-looking member of the opposite sex and you are sixteen again; you stand a little straighter and check your hair. So we have needs, desires, and unresolved issues associated with all of those selves. How old are you when you walk through a bakery and smell freshly baked bread? This same soul can take the role of a parental overseer who decides what is in the best interest of the child. In Act III this guiding parent can be kind and nurturing to the child allowing the TA to experience the joy of simple things. For example, let's consider Bruno.

We met Bruno at a garage sale. Bruno looked like, well . . . Bruno. He wore a T-shirt that revealed his body art and some, shall we say, "interesting" images. As his wife searched through used clothing for a good bargain, Bruno spotted an interesting toy where objects popped out if you pressed the right buttons. It was the kind of gadget that would be recommended for ages two to six.

His wife found several objects that she set aside: clothing, pots, a trivet. All the while, Bruno was mastering his skill with the toy and clearly having a good time. As it often happens, friends are made while discussing garage-sale items. Bruno's wife was soon engaged in a lively conversation with Belle, the person hosting the sale. As the sale was closing, Belle, with a slight wink, asked Bruno's wife, "Will you be getting the toy for the little boy?" The woman looked over at her husband who was still engrossed with the toy and said, "Yes, I will." She packed up the purchases and shouted over to Bruno, "Let's go." When he started to put the toy down, she said "No, don't; I just bought it for you." Bruno replied with a great big grin, "R-e-a-l-l-y?!" Without questioning it for a second, he tucked the toy under his arm and headed for the car. She headed for the driver's side, winking at Belle as she left.

Bruno and his wife knew an important life lesson. At that moment, Bruno's younger self needed to master the toy. He was, in fact, playing. For those of you who may have forgotten what play is, play is undertaking a task that has no practical or useful purpose (as seen through an adult's more logical mind). Play occurs for the enjoyment of the moment. Bruno and his wife understood the need to nurture the child who, though not visible in the five-foot-eleven adult, was clearly there. Onlookers were watching the scenario with joy and understanding. Bruno and his wife had given him permission to "be," and everyone understood how precious a moment it had been.

In this observation, Bruno was the child. And both Bruno and his wife were loving, nurturing parents. Bruno's inside parent could have prevented him from picking up the toy in the first place. His defensive adult may have discarded the gift and said, "Nah, move on." His wife very easily could have said, "Stop wasting time; we need to be at your mother's at noon."

The point is, we need to allow play without judgment. The nurturing parents in our scenario allowed play to happen, increased the bond between husband and wife, and may have resolved a childhood wound of the past. For all we know, a frustration carried forward throughout Bruno's entire adult life may have been resolved that day. It may have opened up creativity. It may have opened up his heart to volunteer as a T-ball coach or be more understanding of his grandchildren.

Nurturing our soul is linked to purpose. Unless we can nurture our soul, we cannot know our purpose because we are denying a part of ourselves.

Now the adults reading this may be saying, "I do not have time to play. Play will not help me accomplish all the things I have to do. We can't all go around playing." We certainly understand. Remember our story about trying to find our definition of fun? Research shows that adult play reduces stress, increases creativity, improves brain function, and helps build our connection with others. Play as adults can have the same benefits that contribute to a child's development.

Let's take a moment to discover how we nurture ourselves with play. Play is not so much what we do, but how we feel as we go about doing it. Your idea of play may differ from someone else's. The following exercise will help you learn from your own history to discover what it is that nurtures your innermost being.

Play is not so much what we do,
but how we feel as we go about doing it.

Act III Memory Play Exercise

In the following exercise, you will begin by remembering the times when you can remember yourself at play. This exercise will help you recognize the emotion of play so that, when you experience the emotion in your day-to-day activities, you will recognize that those activities are your personal definition of play. Start with the earliest memory. What were you doing? Why do you consider it play? How did it make you feel? Try to tie into the feeling and use the memory of the feeling to link to the next memory. If possible, try to move from the earliest memory to the next earliest memory so that you are moving up in age. The following is an example of a memory play exercise.

Exercise Example 8: Act III Memory Play Exercise

Memory	Why is it play?	Feeling
Playing with stuffed toys	I'm talking to my toys, using my imagination.	Comforting, creative, loving
Making mud pies	It's a little forbidden, but I like it.	Joyful, grounded, daring
Playing a toy piano	It is expressive. Sound reacts to my fingers. I enjoy the sense of rhythm.	Grounded, free, in flow
Playing ball	I enjoy watching my skills improve, commanding my body.	Strength, grounded, connected

Creating plays and making puppets	I like making up stories. I like creating things out of nothing.	Creative, clever, fully in the moment, no need to make it good—it is just for today
Making rubber-band guns	I like creating things out of nothing. The activity builds skills. It is somewhat forbidden and I enjoy it with others.	Creative, free-spirited, joyful, gives me a sense of freedom
Sidewalk painting	It's creative; nothing can go wrong because it will fade in a week.	Creative, free-spirited, liberated
Building a skateboard	The skateboard is enjoyed by many. I feel joy when the skateboard works.	Joy of new discovery
Playing basketball	I like the flow of the moment; the ball and I are one.	Flow, connectedness
Solving cryptograms	I feel challenged but there are no grades or requirements. I like solving mysteries.	Being engrossed in the activity, loss of time, joy at accomplishment

Now, you try it.

Act III Memory Play Exercise

Memory	Why is it play?	Feeling

Now, look over your Act III Memory Play Exercise. Do you see a pattern in what you consider fun? Remembering the feeling helps you identify how you may be experiencing it in your own life. Hook into those feelings and list the situations in your own life that re-create those feelings you listed above:

_____

_____

_____

_____

_____

Is your list short or long? Is there anyone in particular who helps you experience the feelings you identified? Do you wish something would change to help you experience more fun? Write those changes down (we can use them in a later exercise).

Goals from the Act III Memory Play Exercise:

_____

_____

_____

_____

_____

See Yourself as Being under the Guidance of God

A 2013 Harris Poll reported that 74% of US adults believed in God. The number may be higher when one considers the "other" names that one has for a higher consciousness, an organizing intelligence, and higher spiritual direction. Modern science is growing in an understanding that the mechanics of nature alone cannot explain the mysteries of our universe, the miracle of our lives, or the synergy of all living things.

We need to feel the connection to that guiding intelligence, which for the sake of simplicity, we will call, "God." Being connected to God helps us recognize that we are like parts of a giant oak tree. The oak's roots are grounded in earth's richness. The trunk stands tall giving strength, direction, nourishment. The branches continue reaching upward and support the leaves. The leaves look toward the sun for nourishment. One leaf may be withering, while another needs more nourishment for growth. One may need to turn more toward the sun. Another is beginning to bud. The tree nourishes all and supports it through all stages of life. One leaf does not say to another "Gee, you should be growing. You should be facing the sun the same direction that I am."

The guiding intelligence of the tree allows each member to be separate yet part of the whole. We are guided by the same. Like the tree, we need to feel the connection to a greater being. We need to know that in our values, we are respected and that we have a place. We need to know that we do not necessarily have to take on the burden of others, because they are protected by the same higher being.

There are three ways of feeling the power and peace of the connection: profound self-love, random acts of kindness, and practicing gratitude.

Profound Self-Love

Profound self-love is the meaning of Act III. Profound self-love comes from accepting yourself with all the flaws, accomplishments, successes, and failures that have come with life. It means forgiving yourself for any wrongdoings or shortcomings, understanding that, at the time, you did the best you could. Loving yourself means that you surround yourself with things that are most beneficial to you. You work on designing your life for your highest good, fulfilling unrealized dreams, providing yourself with opportunities for growing and filling your life with joy. When you love yourself, you naturally extend the same grace to others, and, in doing so, discover the God in all.

Consider the following story. A seventy-four year old contestant appeared in the 2014 auditions of the TV show *America's Got Talent*. He immediately drew the attention of the crowd, at first, because of his age. But as he began singing, the crowd was soon swinging and clapping to the beat as he crooned "I've Got the World on a String." He beamed as the audience became more engaged, naturally commanding the stage. After his performance, one of *AGT*'s judges asked him why he had waited until now to perform publicly. The singer explained that he had a serious stutter, and he had been reluctant to go on stage. He had tended bar for forty-one years, and had retired five years before this performance. But at the moment of his audition, he was a star beyond his biggest dreams. Whether or not he won the competition did not matter, he appeared before a national audience, and had won them over.

Profound self-love is the meaning of Act III.

What was so special about this contestant? No one thought he was "cute." The audience and the judges admired him for his talent and love of life. He had honored his dream of singing—a dream that he had held onto for so many years. He didn't say "It's too late." He honored the desires of his deepest soul, claiming his identity and strength. He chose to give himself the gift of fulfilling his dream in the best way he could. In the light that beamed through his eyes, you could tell that there were no regrets, no "should haves," only the pride and joy of the moment. Everyone connected with him with a secret hope that at seventy-four, they, too, would be living their dreams with the same courageous spirit and the self-love that throws out any restriction that prevents one from living fully.

Many times, we push aside our dreams in order to take care of more pressing needs. We logically conceal the dreams that we believe cannot be fulfilled. Why talk about things that won't happen? We shut down and deny ourselves the opportunity to have or experience what we want most. What are your profound self-love goals? Come on now, we know you have them. A sales training seminar once advised trainees to ask the same question three times. So, what are your profound self-love goals? Still stuck? Then try, "What *might* be a goal?" If all barriers were removed, what might be the goal?

Profound Self-Love Goals:

1._____

2._____

3._____

Mitzvah

We have no idea how great an impact we have on others. A mitzvah is a good deed or an act performed to make someone else feel better. It can have a worldwide impact. You may simply pay for the next car in the drive-through or decide not to shout at the customer service agent who was a little too slow. These acts can have ripple effects. You may never know the chain of events that will or will not happen as a result of your action. But, by knowing you are connected, you will be able to trust in the good effect. That knowing nurtures your soul.

You may never know the chain of events that will or will not happen as a result of your action. But, by knowing you are connected, you will be able to trust in the good effect. That knowing nurtures your soul.

Steve rushed into a local discount store to purchase markers for a presentation. He was pressed for time and chose the shortest checkout line, only to find that the process was taking much longer than he expected. With about fifteen items on the counter, the customer ahead of him was selecting items to remove hoping to get the total bill down. She looked at her little son, who had just grabbed for a box of animal crackers and asked if he could have it. The distracted mother told him to put it back; they were only going to be able to get a few things today because she "forgot" to bring enough money.

117

Steve saw the disappointed look in the boy's face and immediately thought that this would be an opportunity for a mitzvah. Using the mother's excuse as an entry, he said, "I am constantly doing that!" He took out a five-dollar bill and pretended to pick it up off the floor. "Look ma'am, no wonder you are short. This dropped out of your purse! You probably didn't notice it!" The woman looked at the money, then back at her purse. "Are you sure?"

Steve looked at her reassuringly and said, "Yes, it was right here where you dropped it." The woman handed the money to the cashier and finished her transaction, turning around to whisper, "Thank you, have a good day." After the lady was gone, the cashier said, "That was very nice. She lost her husband a year ago and has been having a rough time." Steve had started out to perform an act of kindness, but instead he left feeling full of joy that he had been able to make a difference, if only for a moment.

What good deeds would you consider doing for others?

Mitzvah Goals:

1._____

2._____

3._____

Be Grateful for Your Past, Your Present, and Your Future

Gratitude has been cited by many researchers as contributing to the reduction of stress and the development of well-being. Matthew 6:21 states, "For where your treasure is there will your heart be also." When we are grateful, we acknowledge where our heart is, where our treasures are.

What is gratitude?

When we were interviewing people, we identified and noted many habits and ways of being that categorized emotions. We recognized anger, success, patience, depression, and positivity. But when we tried to find an example of someone who was grateful, our list ran short. Why was this so rare? We have a cultural value that everything we have in life we earned or are entitled to. The picture of someone showing thanks before a meal does not fit with the picture of people who earned their own bread with their own efforts.

Gratitude, or the lack of gratitude, is a habit. When little toddler Sammy starts to pout, the parents know the all too familiar scream that might come next. They ask little Sammy, "Oh, what's wrong? What do you want? What can make you happy?" Soon little Sammy is eating his dessert first, having his ice cream, or staying up for one more TV show. Little Sammy grows up with a belief that unhappiness will lead to gifts intended for his happiness. He fears that the moment he expresses gratitude, the gifts will stop flowing. He is afraid to be happy. He refuses to be grateful.

He focuses on lack. We see this often. Honestly, we all too often do the same thing. We rush to tell people all that is wrong in our lives, hoping that we will earn sympathy and perhaps, a little help or cheering up. Sometimes it works, but there is a much better way.

Jon is a perfect example of someone who trained himself not to be grateful. At the age of fifty-seven, he found himself downsized from his job as a graphic artist for an advertising agency. He spent three years in an unsuccessful job search. All the time, he lamented that he had wasted thirty years of his life at the same company where he never had enough time to be creative in his art. Now, he did not have the money to invest in art supplies or set up a studio. Finally, in a way to protect his dwindling resources, he accepted a job working for his brother who suffered from partial blindness and needed assistance in shopping and small activities around the house.

In his first days of living with his brother, Jon could have won the first-place trophy for being the most negative person. Out of desperation, his brother made a deal with Jon. "I will give you ten dollars a day if you take this spiral-bound notebook. There is one catch: In order to get the ten dollars, you need to write down five things you are grateful for. I will leave a ten-dollar bill on the kitchen table each morning and if you have written down five things in your notebook the day before, the ten dollars is yours to take. I will do this for thirty days."

Jon snickered at the idea, rolled his eyes, and said, "Sure, I'll do that for ten bucks. Okay!"

At first he put down what he thought were silly things. "I have a roof over my head." "I didn't have to eat my brother's cooking tonight." "I saw a good movie on TV." "I am on the coast of Maine." "I found my sunglasses."

He thought, "That was the easiest ten bucks I have ever made." As the days passed, Jon laughed more. Phrases like "this is great," "well that's pretty good," "that was amazing," and "do you remember when..." began to slip into his vocabulary. Inspired by the magnificent scenes of the Maine coast, he was drawn to paint again. He dug some of his old paintings out of storage and placed them in a consignment art gallery. At the end of thirty days his brother asked him if he would like to continue for another thirty days. Jon said, "It's okay." I am not writing them down anymore. Curious, his brother asked, "Why not?" Jon replied, "Because I am thinking about things I am grateful for all the time now." His brother said, "I know what you mean. When I began going blind someone offered me the same deal. I was just paying it forward."

By putting the treasure of his thoughts into gratitude, Jon discovered he was in the perfect situation. He was able to see possibilities, opportunities, and new direction. He placed his treasure where his heart could follow.

We highly recommend you do the same Act III Gratitude Challenge by putting ten dollars (or a small, meaningful amount) in an envelope each day. At day thirty, have your own special celebration!

The format of this exercise is simple:

Act III Gratitude Challenge
DAY 1:

My good news for today is _____.
I am thankful today for _____.
It was really nice of [insert name] to _____.
I had an opportunity to _____.
I didn't have to _____.
I had a conversation with _____.
I was able to _____.

Being grateful has an added benefit. The negatives of the past can turn into positives when you focus on what you learned instead of focusing on what did not go according to plan. You tend to worry less about the future because so much good came out of today. Gratitude makes you feel more connected to a world that is kind, gentle, and giving. Gratitude lessens the burden of being in charge. Being grateful frees you from the false belief that you have to control everything. Good things show up in unexpected places from unexpected people. You are grateful to be able to recognize this. You are able to honestly say, today went well.

Now, what is your good news for today?

1._____

2._____

3._____

Summary

Before continuing on in this book, take a few minutes to reflect on the Nurturing Your Soul topics. In each area below, list your "top three" goals. You will be using these in the last section.

Act III Memory Play Exercise Goals:

1._____

2._____

3._____

Profound Self-Love Goals:

1._____

2._____

3._____

Mitzvah Goals:

1._____

2._____

3._____

What is your good news today? (Gratitude Goals):

1._____

2._____

3._____

Your Act III

God gave energy to youth; maturity to the developing adult; but saved wisdom for the time when one was free to write their third act.

—THE AUTHORS

Taking Your Life Script into Act III

One of the things that we can do to evaluate the script that we have been living, is to examine what has happened to our characters thus far.

For screenwriters, Act III is the most difficult to write. In this act, the main character must conquer his weakness, and maximize the outcome of previous actions. He is at the point of no return. In order to maximize our own character in Act III, we must become a screenwriter. We must weave a story using our own strengths and flaws to build from the story background in Act I and the complexities of Act II. In Act III, the story line climaxes. We have the opportunity now to resolve issues, discard our antagonists, and claim our rewards. Act III has the power to make sense of everything that has happened before; it explains how you used the experiences of the past. How you live Act III will show how you made a difference. Act III explains the purpose of your life.

Act III has the power to make sense of everything
that has happened before; it explains how you
used the experiences of the past.

Let's take some time and set the stage for your Act III. There may be some parts of your script that you need to tear up and write again. There may be other parts that fit perfectly into your storyboard.

Let's get started.

Act I:

This is where characters were introduced and developed.

You are the protagonist of your own story.

Childhood through High School

What are your strongest memories from childhood? We tend to remember moments that defined us. We remember the time that our band won the first-place trophy. We remember we didn't make the debate team. We remember the time we hid from a member of the opposite sex for fear of being rejected. We remember the triumph of getting our first driver's license.

In the following exercise, think back to some of those moments. What are the memories? What characteristics do they bring out as you think of them? Did the experience make you aware of a strength? Write down that characteristic and check the "S" column. Was it a weakness? If so, write it down and check the "W" column. Could it also be an unresolved issue? Then you will need to check the "U" column as well. For triumphs, check the "T" column.

I Recall	Characteristic	S	W	U	T
1. *First day of pre-school*	*Excited about learning*	X	—	—	—
2.		—	—	—	—
3.		—	—	—	—
4.		—	—	—	—
5.		—	—	—	—
6.		—	—	—	—
7.		—	—	—	—
8.		—	—	—	—

What did you learn about your strengths?

Did your unresolved memories reveal a hidden desire?

Do your triumphs remind you of a lost pleasure that might now be a goal?

Act II

Act II is the development of the story lines: the college years, the first jobs, loves lost and found, the starting of families, the triumphs and disappointments, achievements and failures.

The Act II Years

What memories do you recall from your Act II years? Write down the characteristics that emerge from these memories. As you did for Act I, check the "S" column for strengths, the "W" column for weaknesses, the "U" column for unresolved issues, and the "T" column for triumphs. You may certainly check more than one column for each memory.

I Recall	Characteristic	S	W	U	T
1.		—	—	—	—
2.		—	—	—	—
3.		—	—	—	—
4.		—	—	—	—
5.		—	—	—	—
6.		—	—	—	—
7.		—	—	—	—
8.		—	—	—	—

Now, review your Act I and Act II.

What did you learn from your combined experiences?

What do you remember as moments of success or clarity?

What patterns suggest an unresolved issue? Is this something to resolve in Act III or simply something to put to rest?

How can you use your strengths in Act III?

In reviewing your weaknesses, which might be detriments going forward in Act III?

Which weaknesses are irrelevant for Act III?

Value Inventory:

Now look back on your Act I and Act II answers to these questions. You will begin seeing your true character, perhaps you will see where some of your values began.

Patterns of what we consider success, failure, or disappointment frequently reveal what we value most.

Patterns of what we consider success, failure,
or disappointment frequently reveal what we value most.

Take a moment to write a description of your character as you enter your Act III. To help you get started, we have provided a few prompts, leaving you to fill in the blanks.

Act III Character Statement:
I come from a background of _____
_____
_____
_____

And I always knew that _____
_____
_____
_____

I was always afraid of _____
_____
_____
_____

But now that I am older, I _____
_____
_____
_____

Because of this, I _____
_____
_____
_____

Because I know _____
_____
_____

will make me happy.

Writing Act III:

Mentally soar out of your body up one thousand feet and look down at your stage. Write your storyboard for your Act III. How might someone with your strengths, your characteristics, and your desires create the best years of your life?

_____

_____

_____

_____

_____

How might the important unresolved issues get resolved in a positive way? Remember you can only change yourself, you cannot change the other characters as they control their own script.

_____

_____

_____

_____

_____

At the end of each section of this book you listed out your goals. Now is the time to bring all your reflections and plans into your Act III.

My Goals for Act III:

Interests and Dreams:

_____

_____

_____

_____

Technology Needs:

_____

_____

_____

_____

Relevancy Goals:

_____

_____

_____

_____

Relatable Goals:

_____

_____

_____

_____

Currency Goals:

_____

_____

_____

_____

Financial Goals:

_____

_____

_____

_____

Health Test Goals:

_____

_____

_____

_____

Strength and Balance Goals:

_____

_____

_____

_____

Food Choice Goals:

_____

_____

_____

_____

Immunization Goals:

_____

_____

_____

_____

Attitude Goals:

_____

_____

_____

_____

Physical Activity Goals:

_____

_____

_____

_____

Relationship Goals:

_____

_____

_____

_____

Memory Play Exercise Goals:

_____

_____

_____

_____

Profound Self-Love Goals:

_____

_____

_____

_____

Mitzvah Goals:

_____

_____

_____

_____

Gratitude Goals:

_____

_____

_____

_____

You have been through an intense journey through this book exploring the major areas of recognizing and fulfilling dreams, work and financial management, and relationships. You have delved into establishing your interests, have identified goals to stay in touch with technology, to improve your health, and to nurture your soul. You have mapped out your storyboard and identified people who you will want to have with you in your Act III and understand what you seek in new relationships.

Now what steps can you take in the next three months to get you moving in the direction that you have chosen? Remember, this is your Act III and you are the lead character. Many people worry that they must seek approval from others. But remember, if the significant people in your life truly love and support you, they will want nothing more than to see you happily supporting your dreams.

Remember the Kaizen principle and take it one step at a time. Many make the mistake thinking that their transition must be on a grand scale. Remember what we talked about earlier, you never know the full impact of a single action. It could be great or small.

We invite you to tell us about the ways in which you have used this book to reach the dreams that you have uncovered and the opportunities that you have found along the way. Visit us at *myact3.com* and share your story with us. Get to know us, respond to the blogs, take the current Act III quiz and enjoy your morning tea or coffee.

EPILOGUE

In Celebration of Act III

Carl Jung, the father of existential psychology, defined our lives as composed of two major developmental stages. The first stage, our "junior" stage, was dedicated to developing the strengths and experiences of the hero. The hero's journey begins at the onset of adulthood. The youth is bored with the ho-hum of his village or the young hero is hiding in a schoolroom still unwilling to reveal his powers. The young girl is dutifully fulfilling the role of a daughter. Then, the opportunity comes when he (or she) needs to leave home to fight the war, to challenge the enemy, or sail the seas in search of an adventurous mission. During the process, the hero builds his strengths and secures his ego. But along the way, there is a fatal flaw that is disclosed. The hero is beset with problems. Perhaps there is failure in battle or a betrayal by the second in command.

The ship is crushed in a storm or the hero learns that he cannot save his best friend. These disappointments must be dealt with. Perhaps the hero must start over, rebuilding the ruined ship; perhaps he must deal with his sorrow. In the end, if he is truly a hero, he discovers that he can overcome his calamities, obstacles, setbacks, and trials to complete the mission. He discovers that his strength is even greater than he had imagined. In the end, he is able to return home. But what happens next? The hero seems to slip into a "happy ever after."

The hero has entered the second half of his development. He has been humbled; he knows that his strength has come from failure.

He has entered the age of wisdom.

We of Act III are finalizing our own journey. We may still be in the battle or we may still be struggling with the challenges of the warrior. If we are very, very fortunate, we have entered the age of wisdom. Because of our failures, we are more empathetic with others. Because we have erred, we are more willing to forgive. Because we have come back from disappointments, we can encourage. Because we have known sorrow, we can console. We have been through our stages. We have worn bandanas around our foreheads, pushed a little too hard, worn ridiculous hairdos in an effort to express our individuality and at the top of our success, discovered that it was not what we wanted.

We have entered our age of wisdom.

Now, when we see our grandson with shorts barely hanging on to his "um um ums" or our granddaughter with a ring through her nose and a tattoo on the side of her neck, we see these acts of rebellion as ordinary stages of growing up. We can embrace our young heroes knowing that there are no hard-core rights or wrongs, but that love and relationship—and family—are more precious than the details. What's more, we can patiently console our own adult children, knowing that their struggles in life are equally about their own development on their path. Our role is to provide patience, understanding, and on rare occasions, guidance. We can offer the one or two comments that our juniors can use when they need it—when they know enough to understand.

We have entered the age of wisdom.

Our sacred prize of understanding is shared only with those who have shared the same experiences. If you meet with a fellow companion in the age of wisdom who complains of the ignorance around him, we need merely remind him or her of the secret wisdom: "He is thirty years old." The understanding meets and you hear, "Yeah, I remember."

We are adaptable and resilient. We have learned that success can turn to failure and that failure can give birth to triumph. We have seen change again and again and accept that those who follow us need to try again. We wish them well.

Our ninety-year-old friend Mabel told us that we were *so* young. She assured us that no one understood what life was about until they were at least eighty.

If she is right, then the journey ahead should be glorious.

REFERENCE PAGES

Following is a list of individuals, organizations, products, studies, and websites mentioned in our book as representations of the baby boomer culture. We would like to acknowledge them below:

INDIVIDUALS

Betty White in 2010, at eighty-eight years of age, hosted Saturday Night Live. It was a true showstopper.

Carl Jung, founder of analytical psychology, developed the concepts of archetypes and the collective unconscious. His books include The Red Book (2009), Man and His Symbols (1964), and Memories, Dreams, Reflections (1963).

Confucius was a fourth century BC Chinese teacher, politician, and philosopher.

Charles H. Duell was Commissioner of the US Patent and Trademark Office, 1891-1901.

Eubie Blake, born James Hubert Blake, was an American composer and lyricist. His compositions include "I'm Just Wild About Harry." The musical Eubie featured a compilation of his works.

John Barrymore, born 1882, was an actor remembered for his interpretations of Shakespeare, a true American icon of cinema and stage.

John Maynard Keynes is the father of Keynesian economic theory and a reknown philosopher. The quote used is from the prelude to The General

Theory of Employment, Interest and Money (1936), published by Palgrave Macmillan.

Paramahansa Yogananda is the founder of Self-Realization Fellowship and recognized spiritual leader. The quote has been attributed to him by multiple sources.

Peace Pilgrim (1908-1981) was born Mildred Lisette Norman. She walked 25,000 miles over a 28-year period on a mission for peace and a meaningful way of life.

ORGANIZATIONS

America's Got Talent is a registered trademark of FremantleMedia North America & Simco, Ltd., 2014.

Center for Disease Control focuses on health, safety, and security threats in the US and throughout the world. For more information go to www.cdc.gov.

Federal Reserve Bank of St. Louis. Federal Reserve Economic Data can be found at http://research.stlouisfed.org.

Saturday Night Live is broadcasted from NBC Headquarters and celebrated its 40th Season in September 2014.

Social Security Administration hosts the retirement estimator at http://www.ssa.gov/retire2/estimator.htm.

PRODUCTS

BlackBerry is a product of BlackBerry Limited, a Canadian telecommunications and wireless equipment company.

Montblanc has been known for its fine writing instruments since 1924. The company's pens are among the most famous of our generation.

Mr. Holland's Opus was a 1995 film directed by Stephen Herek, produced by Ted Field, Robert W. Cort, and Michael Nolin and written by Patrick Sheane Duncan.

PowerPoint is a product of Microsoft Corporation.

The Oxford Dictionary is copyrighted by the Oxford University Press.

Virginia Slims was manufactured by the Altria Group and was introduced in 1968 with the intention of capturing the emerging young professional female market.

STUDIES AND SURVEYS

2013 Harris Poll Survey. Additional information on this survey can be found on www.harrisinteractive.com.

Food for Thought: An Epigenetic Guide to Wellness by George Febish and Jo Anne Oxley.

Kaizen is a method of continuous improvement popularized in Japan and spread throughout the world.

National Council on Aging has conducted annual surveys of Americans 60 years of age and older since 2012. Additional survey results can be found at www.ncoa.org. USA Today has been one of the sponsors.

Tony Buzan is considered the father of modern mind mapping. More information can be found at www.tonybuzan.com.

WEBSITES

Dropbox.com is a cloud-based storage service allowing companies and individuals to collaborate by shared storage and secured access to files.

eBay.com is an Internet site for selling and auctioning products.

Facebook.com is a popular social networking site.

http://thescriptlab.com is a website designed for the creative industry of writers and filmmakers providing screenwriting resources and entertainment news.

Meetup.com is a website for people to share their interests and form offline clubs. Meetup groups are established in local communities worldwide.

YouTube.com is an Internet site for sharing videos on a variety of topics. The site was created by three PayPal employees in February 2005.